The Colonial Harem

Theory and History of Literature
Edited by Wlad Godzich and Jochen Schulte-Sasse

The Colonial Harem

Malek Alloula

Translation by
Myrna Godzich and Wlad Godzich

Introduction by
Barbara Harlow

Theory and History of Literature, Volume 21

University of Minnesota Press
Minneapolis
London

Published by the University of Minnesota Press,
111 Third Avenue South, Suite 290, Minneapolis, MN 55401-2520.
Printed in the United States of America on acid-free paper.
Designed by Gwen M. Willems.
Eighth printing, 2017

Library of Congress Cataloging-in-Publication Data
Alloula, Malek.
    The colonial harem.

    (Theory and history of literature ; v. 21)
    Translation of: Le harem colonial.
    Bibliography: p.
    1. Women–Algeria–Social conditions. 2. Postal cards–Algeria. 3. Photography of women.
4. Harem.
I. Title. II. Series.
HQ1791.5.A7613   1986   305.4'0965   85-16527
ISBN 978-0-8166-1383-0
ISBN 978-0-8166-1384-7 (pbk.)

*This essay, which owes much
to Wardiya and to Hayyem,
is dedicated to the memory of
Roland Barthes*

Contents

Introduction

Scene 60. Blockade rue de la Lyre. Outside. Day.

Djamila is tense, pale, her features are strained. Her eyes seem even larger with make-up. Now, at the blockade at rue de la Lyre the Casbah exit is blocked. An Algerian has been discovered without documents. He argues, shouts, and says that he wants to go back.

Incoherent Voices.

The soldiers try to catch him, he struggles to get free. Meanwhile the people push forward in protest. Two soldiers catch the Algerian and drag him bodily into the guard posts. The flow of people continues.
Djamila steps forward, holding the cosmetic-case with both of her hands. She doesn't know how to carry it, and from time to time she changes her position. She realizes that she looks awkward. It's now her turn. The soldiers' tone is arrogant. The previous scene has made them nervous. An officer signals her to pass, then points to the cosmetic-case.

Officer: What's inside?

Instinctively, Djamila lifts the case and looks at it; she feels herself failing, but makes an effort to answer.

Djamila: Here?

Officer: There . . .

Djamila uses all her strength to smile and she succeeds. Her eyes light up defiantly.

Djamila (provocatively): Nothing.

The officer signals her to pass.

    (From the film *The Battle of Algiers*, directed by Gillo Pontecorvo, 1966.)[1]

Djamila, a young Algerian woman, is a member of Algeria's National Liberation Front (FLN). Her cosmetic bag, which she holds so awkwardly under the gaze of the French soldiers as she leaves the Arab quarter of Algiers (the Casbah, or *madina*) to enter the French section (or *ville nouvelle*) of the city, contains explosives destined for the milk bar in the rue d'Isly. It is 1956 and the Battle of Algiers is about to begin. Djamila, like many other Arab women in her country, has assumed a role in her social order, one which not only has brought her out of seclusion in the home and into the streets but has refashioned her physical and cultural appearance. She has become a part of the Algerian revolution. Her eyes, which according to the traditional and especially Western image of the Arab woman were alone visible behind an all-concealing veil, are now large with mascara. Her face and hair are exposed. The veil is gone and has been replaced by Western clothes. The makeup, however, and the short skirt have, paradoxically, become part of the Algerian resistance to French colonialism. Whereas it was the veil that had previously taken on a symbolic significance as an assertion of tradition and custom in Algeria, it was Western apparel that early in the revolution allowed Algerian women, like Djamila, to actively confront the colonial presence in the streets. Later, toward the end of the revolution, when Western-clad Algerian women became suspect, the veil was once

again assumed by the women of the FLN so that they could conceal within its folds the weapons and explosive devices they carried between the French and Arab quarters of the city. There is, according to Frantz Fanon's *A Dying Colonialism*, his study of the Algerian revolution, a "historic dynamism of the veil," which can be perceived over the course of France's colonization of Algeria.

In the beginning, the veil was a mechanism of resistance, but its value for the social group remained very strong. The veil was worn because tradition demanded a rigid separation of the sexes, but also because the occupier was bent on unveiling Algeria. In a second phase, the mutation occurred in connection with the Revolution and under special circumstances. The veil was abandoned in the course of revolutionary action. What had been used to block the psychological or political offensives of the occupier became a means, an instrument. The veil helped the Algerian woman to meet the new problems created by the struggle.[2]

In *The Colonial Harem*, Malek Alloula has collected, arranged, and annotated the picture postcards of Algerian women produced and sent by the French in Algeria during the first three decades of this century. This Algerian writer's study of the postcards, which reveals an intense preoccupation with the veiled female body, engages historically in the same kind of social practice that the anthropologist Pierre Bourdieu has termed "challenge and riposte." Bourdieu examined this dialectic in the context of Kabylian society, a Berber population in Algeria among whom he worked and where the exchange of challenges served to maintain the tribal sense of honor. "The nature of the riposte," according to Bourdieu, "makes the challenge a challenge, as opposed to mere aggression."[3] *The Colonial Harem* presents a literary-historical version of riposte to the challenge of French colonialism which, despite independence, has continued to influence present-day Algeria. To understand the nature of that riposte, it must be examined in the context of French-Algerian relations and against the background of East-West contacts. The role played by women, both real and imaginary, has been critical to these encounters. Furthermore, despite the numerous studies being done on the Western vision of the Orient, or, in its broadest terms, of the Other,[4] the corresponding vision or viewpoint of the so-called Oriental, the Arab or the Algerian, with regard to the West[5] has received little systematic attention. Alloula's commentary on the postcards provides such a perspective. The perspective also displays the historical tension produced by technological disparities and the discrepancies of unequal development. "A reading of the sort that I propose to undertake," Alloula writes, "would be entirely superfluous if there existed photographic traces of the gaze of the colonized upon the colonizer. In their absence, that is, in the absence of a confrontation of opposed gazes, I attempt here, lagging far behind History, to return this immense postcard to its sender." (p 5) Although the postcards in this book are from the early twentieth century, they do not represent a historically isolable phenomenon. They are part of a conflict whose consequences continue to interest contemporary global politics and which has important ramifications in the intellectual arena as well.

Pontecorvo's film *The Battle of Algiers* was produced in 1966, four years after the Algerian revolution had ended, culminating in the establishment of an independent Algerian state following more than a century of French colonial domination. Five years after its release, the film was still banned in France, where the *pieds noirs*, the former French settlers of Algeria, continued to protest the showing of the internationally acclaimed film. The Algerian revolution, which lasted eight violent years, from November 1954 to July 1962, had sharply polarized French public opinion and policy at the same time that it posed serious problems for European intellectuals and leftists. The Algerian resistance was accused of terrorism, and the French were charged with torture in their treatment of prisoners. The protracted debate that ensued over armed resistance and loyalty to the mother country obliged prominent literary figures to take sides, often against each other.

Albert Camus, himself a *pied noir* who left Algeria in 1939, continued to believe in 1958 in maintaining a French Algeria. Camus, whose influence in the West derived both from his role in the French resistance during World War II and from his position within the existentialist movement, opposed in his political writings and statements at the time not only the tactics but the goal of the Algerian nationalists. In the introduction to his collected essays on Algeria, *Actuelles III*, Camus condemned the FLN and advocated French commitment to a French Algeria: "The struggle of ideas is possible, even if armed, and it is right to recognize the enemy's reasons before defending oneself against him. On both sides, nonetheless, terror, however long it might last, changes the order of the terms. When one's own family is in immediate danger of death, one might want to make it more generous and more just, one should even continue to do so, but (and make no mistake here!) without failing in the solidarity owing in such danger in order that the family at least survive and in surviving discover the chance to be just."[6] Camus concluded his introduction by clarifying his sense of a fair solution to the Algerian question: "An Algeria constituted of federated settlements and tied to France seems to me preferable, without any possible comparison to simple justice, to an Algeria tied to an empire of Islam which would only bring about an increase of misery and suffering and uproot the French people of Algeria from their native country."[7]

Whereas Camus condemned the FLN for its use of terror as a tactic in its armed struggle against colonialism and insisted on Algeria as a French possession, Simone de Beauvoir challenged the French regime for its use of torture against suspected partisans of the resistance movement. In the case of Djamila Boupacha, "an Algerian girl of 23, an FLN liaison agent, [was] illegally imprisoned by French military forces, who subjected her to torture and deflowered her with a bottle."[8] When this case was brought before the French public in 1961, de Beauvoir became active in the attempt to gain a hearing for the young woman. In her introduction to the account by Djamila's lawyer of her client's torture and the efforts to win her release, the French feminist wrote: "From 1954 onwards we have all compounded our consciences with a species of racial extermination that—first in the name of 'subjugating rebellious elements' and later in that of 'pacification'—has claimed over a million victims."[9]

Djamila was released from prison in 1962 when general amnesty was granted at the end of the war. The charges of torture that she had brought against the French army in Algeria were thus never heard, nor was her case decided by a court of law. Three years earlier, in 1959, however, Ahmed Taleb Ibrahimi, now a minister in the Algerian government, but at that time a young Algerian held in the French prison at Fresnes for subversive activities against the state, addressed an open letter to Albert Camus in which he rejected the former French settler's appeals for solidarity. Ahmed Taleb, who as a lycéen in Algeria had read and admired Camus's writings, now wrote:

It is strange to note that you who proclaimed your love for your Arab "brothers" should display such an arrogant contempt for everything Arab, Muslim and Oriental. You, who pretend that Algeria is your "true country," are totally ignorant of its heritage even to the point of speaking of Algerian cities "without a past" [from L'été]. Even the most superficial knowledge of the history of the Maghrib would have shown you that the Algerian nation is not an epiphenomenon and that its destiny, even if it is Mediterranean, is also African and Arab.[10]

Algeria's revolution ended finally in the creation of a socialist government with Islam as the state religion and Arabic as the official language. Algeria today holds membership in the Arab League, the Organization of African Unity (OAU), the Organization of the Islamic Conference (OIC), and the Non-Aligned Countries.

In *The Colonial Harem*, there are both French and Algerian spectators:

Alloula, an Algerian, is examining French observations of Algeria. Like the "sentimental spectator" of Barthes's *Camera Lucida*, Alloula examines these postcards not only as "a question (a theme) but as a wound."[11] And yet, unlike Barthes, who believed in the principle "never to reduce myself-as-subject, confronting certain photographs, to the disincarnated, disaffected *socius* which science is concerned with,"[12] Alloula recognizes in his own vision the influence of a *socius*, neither disincarnated nor disaffected but historically conditioned: "What I read on these cards does not leave me indifferent. It demonstrates to me, were that still necessary, the desolate poverty of a gaze that I myself, as an Algerian, must have been the object of at some moment in my personal history. Among us, we believe in the nefarious effects of the evil eye (the evil gaze). We conjure them with our hand spread out like a fan. I close my hand back upon a pen to write *my* exorcism: *this text*." (p. 5) Alloula's conjuring act challenges the reader-critic of his book to consider the historical consequences of these artifacts of popular culture.

The postcards present thirty years of French colonial presence in Algeria and illustrate its distorting effects on Algerian society. In the end, the French conquest of Algeria, begun in 1830 and depicted in certain of its aspects on these postcards, was less a conquest than a deformation of the social order. Through a demystifying reorganization of the photos, Alloula points out one of the modes of that deformation: the photographer's studio and the native models who reenact exotic rituals in costumes provided by the picture-taking impresario. The postcards, in the context of *The Colonial Harem*, no longer represent Algeria and the Algerian woman but rather the Frenchman's phantasm of the Oriental female and her inaccessibility behind the veil in the forbidden harem. Malek Alloula's study can on one level be compared to the Arab's attack on Meursault and Raymond in Camus's novel *The Stranger*, in which the Arab trespasses into the world of the *colons* in order to save the honor of his sister. As Bourdieu maintains, however, "to reduce to the function of communication phenomena such as the dialectic of challenge and riposte, and more generally, the exchange of gifts, words and women, is to ignore the structural ambivalence which predisposes them to fulfill a political function of domination in and through performance of the communication function."[13] The background of French-Algerian relations within the larger setting of the history of the East-West conflict is critical to the assessment of these postcards.

The French, during their colonization of the Maghrib, did not produce postcards exclusively of women in Algeria; a series of architectural representations of mosques, traditional houses, tombs, and fountains, highlighted by arabesques and *polygones étoilés*, might also provide material for cultural and ideological scrutiny.[14] Landscape views are likewise of interest in cases where possession and occupation of the land are at stake.[15] Women, however, have long been at the center of the conflict between East and West, not only as partisans in the FLN, a role which had problematic consequences within Algerian society, but also as phantasmic representations of Western designs on the Orient. The misunderstandings of the woman's place and role in the respective societies have continued through the centuries to scar relations between the different cultures. Herodotus, writing in the fifth century B.C., already had assigned primary importance to women in his account of the Persian Wars.

Hitherto the injuries on either side had been mere acts of common violence; but in what followed the Persians consider that the Greeks were greatly to blame, since before any attack had been made on Europe, they led an army into Asia. Now, as for the carrying off of women, it is the deed, they say, of a rogue; but to make a stir about such as are carried off, argues a man a fool. Men of sense care nothing for such women, since it is plain that without their own consent they would never be forced away. The Asiatics, when the Greeks ran off with their women, never troubled themselves about the matter; but the Greeks, for the sake of a single

Lacedaemonian girl, collected a vast armament, invaded Asia, and destroyed the kingdom of Priam. Hence they ever looked upon the Greeks as their open enemies.[16]

Later, a major thrust of the medieval European attack on Islam was an *argumentum ad hominem* directed at the alleged promiscuity of its Prophet, Muhammad, who was criticized for indulging in polygamy. Even his followers, who were allowed just four wives and only if each could be equitably provided for, were similarly castigated. In the Koran, however, Allah had admonished the Muslim believers, "If you fear that you will not act justly towards the orphans, marry such women as seem good to you, two, three, four; but if you fear you will not be equitable, then only one, or what your right hands own; so it is likelier you will not be partial."[17]

The question whether Islam and its social organization of men and women represented a significant improvement over previous family patterns and customary tribal law in nomadic Arabia at the time of Muhammad (seventh century A.D.) continues to be debated by scholars, feminists and theologians, Muslim and non-Muslim alike. Especially in recent decades, that is, in the period following independence, the various Arabic and Islamic countries, such as Egypt, Jordan, Morocco, Tunisia, Algeria, and South Yemen, have promulgated legal reforms designed to improve the social and personal status of women in society. These reforms, which still require more stringent efforts in their implementation, have addressed in particular issues of arranged marriage, inheritance, dowry, polygamy, and divorce (*talaq*).[18] The popular image of slave girls, harems, and concubines nonetheless continued to horrify and titillate Western critics of the Muslim world throughout the colonial period. An essential part of Gérard de Nerval's "Voyage en Orient" in the mid-nineteenth century, for example, was his marriage to a Druze woman in Lebanon after the relationship with his slave girl in Cairo had failed.[19] Less than a century later, Meursault, the protagonist in Camus's 1939 novel, *The Stranger*, killed an Algerian Arab who refused to make his sister available to the French colonialists.[20] Possession of Arab women came to serve as a surrogate for and means to the political and military conquest of the Arab world.

The necessary connection between phantasm and political agenda is identified and illustrated in Malek Alloula's presentation of the French colonial postcard. "The Orient," he writes, "is no longer the dreamland. Since the middle of the nineteenth century, it has inched closer. Colonialism makes a grab for it, appropriates it by dint of war, binds it hand and foot with myriad bonds of exploitation and hands it over to the devouring appetite of the great mother countries, ever hungry for raw materials." (p. 3)

More than analogy links the imperialist project of colonizing other lands and peoples with the phantasm of appropriation of the veiled, exotic female. The similarity between penetrating the secret, tantalizing recesses of the harem and making the masqueraded pilgrimage to Mecca and the holy Kaaba of Islam, which nineteenth-century travelers like Sir Richard Burton and A. Kinglake did, [21] reveals the many guises under which imperialism penetrated the Arab world. During the First World War, T. E. Lawrence claimed to champion the Arab cause, thus earning Arab robes and the title "Lawrence of Arabia", but at the Paris conference following the war, he refused to support their demands for the independent Arab kingdom that their British and French allies had promised them in return for their support against the Germans and the Turks. Britain and France instead divided the spoils between themselves, leaving only the area of Palestine to be contested in a later struggle.

France's colonization of Algeria, however, had begun in 1830 when the French sent a military expedition to that country following a quarrel involving insult and financial debts between the Turkish dey of Algiers and the French consul in the city. A combination of domestic politics, competition with England over land and influence in Africa and the Arab world, and imperial designs of its own then led France to embark on a policy of conquest in Algeria. [22] The resistance to the French invasion led by Abd al-Qadir, who descended from a leading family of marabouts, or holy men, collapsed in 1847 when the Amir surrendered to the French. In 1857, Kabylia was subjugated and the French conquest of Algeria was complete.

The military invasion of Algeria was accompanied in the meantime by colonial settlement, and by 1870 nearly 250,000 *colons* had appropriated 674, 340 hectares of farmland and 160,000 hectares of forestland. Under Roman influence and later under Ottoman control, the production of wheat had been encouraged in Algeria, as in the rest of North Africa, which contributed significantly to the food supply of the Mediterranean. One effect of the French colonization of North Africa was to shift the use of the land from wheat crops to viniculture, not only an abuse of the soil, which is now so depleted as to make a return to wheat and grain production almost impossible, but an offense as well against indigenous Muslim practice, which prohibits the drinking of wine. The Islamic judiciary was suppressed, and the French policy of *cantonnement* confined the indigenous population to specific areas. A series of laws continued to make traditional tribal lands available to the *colons* for cultivation and settlement. According to Abdallah Laroui, a Moroccan historian:

The history of Algeria from 1830 to 1871 is made up of pretenses: the colons who allegedly wished to trans-

form the Algerians into men like them-selves, when in reality their only desire was to transform the soil of Algeria into French soil; the military, who suppos-edly respected the local traditions and way of life, whereas in reality their only interest was to govern with the least possible effort; the claim of Napo-leon III that he was building an Arab kingdom, whereas his central ideas were the "Americanization" of the French economy and the French coloni-zation of Algeria. [23]

Tensions between Algerian Arabs and French settlers intensified, especially after World War I. Of the 173,000 Algerian Muslims who served in the French army, 25,000 lost their lives. Since their loyalty to France was neither recognized nor rewarded, and since the French government continued to respond to the settlers' pressure for disenfranchisement of the Muslim population, Algerian nationalist sentiment began to find expression in various political movements and organizations. The Young Algerians, which was formed in 1919 and counted Farhat 'Abbas among its leaders, sought assimilation into France on terms of equality. In 1926, the Etoile Nord-Africaine was founded by Messali al-Hajj to coordinate activities of the North African workers in France. Both of these men would later be active in the Algerian revolution, although neither of them initially supported the FLN. Farhat 'Abbas, who eventually negotiated independence on behalf of the FLN, continued to seek reform rather than revolution, and Messali al-Hajj formed his own Mouvement National Algérien (MNA). On 1 November 1954 the Algerian revolution broke out and the French government responded by sending additional troops to reinforce its army of 50,000 soldiers already in Algeria.

The nationalism that emerged in the early decades of the twentieth century had begun as a demand by Algerians for full rights as French citizens without surrendering their personal status as Muslims. Even this agenda, however, proved threatening to the French sense of their own cultural and political superiority, and they undertook a program of active efforts to divert and neutralize any tendency to develop an independent Algerian national identity. With the suppression and neglect of Arab schools, education had already become the domain of the French, and Algerian Arabs were schooled, if at all, in French language, history, and culture. Those students who succeeded according to French standards were described by the French as *évolués*. Many of the intellectuals—like Shakespeare's Caliban, whose profit from learning the English language was that he now "knew how to curse"—went on to become leaders in the independence movement. At the same time, however, France's "civilizing mission" in Algeria produced what Malek Haddad described in a speech in Beirut in 1961 as "the most perfidious case of depersonalization in history, a case of cultural asphyxia."[24] This cultural tension is still evident today in the problems encountered by the Algerian government's ongoing program of Arabization in education, in the bureaucracy, and in daily life. Many of the most prominent Algerian writers, like their Tunisian and Moroccan counterparts, indeed like Malek Alloula himself, an Algerian living in France, continue to write in French, a practice which remains central to the contemporary Maghrib's literary debate. On the one hand, to write in French is criticized as continued submission to the literary and ideological influence of the former colonizer. Abdelkebir Khatibi, the Moroccan writer and critic, maintains, on the other hand, in his study *Le Roman maghrébin*, that the use of the French language by North African writers can produce a kind of "irony which would not only be a form of revenge on the part of the colonized who had been oppressed and seduced by the West, but would also allow the francophone North African writer to distance himself with regard to the language by inverting it, destroying it, and presenting new structures such that the French reader would become a stranger in his own language."[25]

"In the colonialist program," according to Frantz Fanon, "it was the woman who was given the historic mission of shaking up the man."[26] Although education was one method the French used to assimilate what threatened to develop as a progressive Algerian consciousness, too extensive an assimilation would have been counterproductive, and thus French policy also included the systematic subversion of the Algerian social structure, traditions, and habits. Such a program was not unique to the French. The British too had attempted in India and Africa to collaborate with the women under the pretext of liberating them from oppression by their own men: "brown women saved by white men from brown men," as Gayatri Spivak formulates the practice in her analysis of widow sacrifice, or suttee, in India and the British colonial efforts to intervene and allegedly reform the custom.[27] Similarly, in Kenya, in the 1920s, British missionaries were active in instigating the Christianizing campaign against the tradition of female circumcision. In his novel *The River Between*,[28] the Kenyan writer Ngugi wa Thiong'o describes the dilemma created by British interference and co-optation for those who wished to reform the society from within. Kikuyu women in Kenya at that time began to demand the right to womanhood through circumcision as an assertion of their Kenyan identity against the British imperialists. Fanon has analyzed an analogous case in Algeria:

The officials of the French administration in Algeria, committed to destroying the people's originality, and under instructions to bring about the disintegration, at whatever cost, of forms of existence likely to evoke a national reality directly or indirectly, were to concentrate their efforts on the wearing of the veil, which was looked upon at this juncture as a symbol of the status of the Algerian woman.[29]

As would happen later in Iran during the Khomeini-led revolution against the Shah's dictatorship, Algerian women collectively reassumed the veil, which previously had been predominantly an urban phenomenon, redefining it first as a symbolic, and later as a practical, instrument in their resistance to French domination.

The French found an independent Algerian Arab social order compromising to their political and cultural hegemony over the country, and their concern with the existence and historical dynamic of that order was largely negative. Their program, when not calculated to maximize exploitation, was the suppression of indigenous customs. The neglect for which Ahmed Taleb had reproached Camus, who wrote of Algerian cities "sans passé," is evident as well in the writings of other literary French travelers to the North African coast. Their texts demonstrate the larger biases of the time. In *Amyntas*, his collection of travel writings from North Africa at the turn of the century, André Gide describes his enamored response to the country and the utter "nothingness" he discovers there. "There was a time," he writes,

when I dared not admit to myself how little refuge and nourishment art can find on this soil. I needed to pretend it was beautiful before daring to admire it so passionately. It was in the days when I willingly confused art and nature. Now, what I like in this land is, I am well aware, its very hideousness, its intemperate climate: what compels all art not *to exist . . . or to take refuge elsewhere.*[30]

Michel, the hero of Gide's *L'Immoraliste*, displays the same refusal to recognize in the Algerian landscape the life and historical presence of a people. The children, whom the ailing Michel had met on his first visit to Biskra, are no longer interesting to him on the occasion of his second encounter, when he finds them to have grown two years older and to have developed new activities and habits binding them to the social life of the oasis. Bachir is now washing dishes in a cafe; Ashour is employed breaking stones on the highway; still another is selling bread; Agib has become a butcher; Boubaker is married. "And was this all that remained?" Michel responded to the changes in the Algerian youths, "All that life had made of them?"[31] The children's very claim to a historicity of their own is anathema to Gide's aestheticism.

In *The Stranger*, Camus described the violent intervention of Meursault and his compatriot Raymond into Algerian society but never recognized, acknowledged, or even named it as a society with its own internal structure, mores, and contradictions. The postcards presented in *The Colonial Harem* produce a similar effect. They wrest certain features of Algerian life from their indigenous context only to reinscribe them within a framework that answers to the political and psychological needs of the imperialist's appropriation of the Orient. The series of postcards assembled in the chapter entitled "Couples" purport, for example, to represent Algerian life, not in the harem, which the Orientalist has already isolated from its place in the home, but in its domestic setting. For the producers and consumers of the images, "the Algerian couple is," Alloula comments, "just as counterfeitable as the rest for the sake of the cause." (p. 37) The imposition of the Western couple as the model for family relations on a society that depends for the strength of its fabric on kinship and an extended family network serves, as the commentary maintains, to "break up the very kernel of the resistance to colonial penetration: the traditional family." (p. 39)

As the Algerian novelist Rachid Boudjedra claims, "in Muslim societies, there is one reserved, almost taboo, domain: the domain constituted by the problems of the family." The photographer's entry into the home, with its highly developed organization of space consonant with an evolved social order,[32] extends the militant offensive of the colonial male's intrusion into the protected space of the harem. Each violation reenacts the colonial phantasm of exploitation and appropriation.[33] The Algerian nationalist response, however, radically altered the picture. When the French were challenged, not by the local appropriations of ethnically exclusive filial loyalties they had sought to exploit, but by the progressive affiliations of a resistance movement, they, like Gide's Michel, turned to refuge in the sheltering bosom of their motherland. Kateb Yacine, an Algerian writer, accepts no excuse for such an attitude, which he sees epitomized in Camus's capitulation to power:

At one time he was the friend of the people. This was understandable during the period of paternalism when the power of the popular front had not yet come into being. But this popular front is now present and he is afraid; he hides himself behind attitudes such as: if I had to choose between justice and my mother, I would pick my mother.[34]

The concern with genealogy and lineage in modern Algerian novels, from Kateb Yacine's *Nedjma* (1956), dealing with the disarray produced by the mixed marriage between an Algerian Berber and a Frenchwoman, to Rachid Boudjedra's *Les 1001 années de la nostalgie* (1979), which responds to the effects of pan-Arab nationalism, testifies to the larger literary project undertaken by contemporary Maghrib writers. Such a project contends with the necessity of reworking the lost order of the past into a future vision. That vision must not only restore the interrupted history but reorient it in terms that take into account the intervening developments of colonialism, revolution, and independence, as well as the combined influences of the Third World and the former colonial mother, France. Access to the archives of history, which include oral tradition, written narratives, photographs, and the documents and artifacts of the past, and the assumption of a historical role are equally critical to this project. The popular memory must be restored but not without a radical reexamination of the cultural and political values that sustained the colonial enterprise in its attempted suppression of that memory through an enactment of its own fantasies of power.

Abdelkebir Khatibi comments in his study of North Africa, *Maghreb pluriel*, on the historical coincidence of *deconstruction* and *decolonization*.[35] In *The Colonial Harem*, Malek Alloula elicits the combined force of the two tasks from the point of view of the formerly colonized subject. His choice of the harem as *topos* suggests the various fronts, cultural and political, on which the struggle has been played out and the arena in which his own discourse will stand. Like the unnamed Arab in *The Stranger*, Alloula challenges the aggressor of his countrywomen, but that challenge necessitates an elaboration of the terms to be used in the confrontation. The commonplace of the harem, essential as a product of the Western imagination and as a socialized fea-

ture of the Eastern world, demands a reciprocal reorganization of the relations of power. "Above and beyond the anecdote which ornaments it, the 'harem connection' betrays its deep affinity with an Occident which is beginning to question the principles of its political institutions, the aims of education, the role of the family, the enigma of the relations between the sexes—all questions which involve, even more profoundly than may appear, the essence of its metaphysics."[36]

Women writers of the Maghrib have already offered searching critiques of their contemporary societies and their historical conditioning. These writers, like Fatima Mernissi from Morocco in *Beyond the Veil: Male-Female Dynamics in a Modern Muslim Society* and the Algerian Fadela M'rabet in her essays "La Femme algérienne" and "Les Algériennes," have broached an area of interrogation from within their own traditions that calls into question not only tradition, convention, and religion but the modern uses of power in postindependence North Africa as well. Assia Djebar's series of *histoires, Les Femmes d'Alger dans leur appartement*, "translates," she says, the polyphonic memory of the contemporary Algerian woman. "But from what language? From Arabic? From a popular Arabic, or a feminine Arabic? One might as well say, from a subterranean Arabic,"[37] Djebar evokes the heroines of Algerian history: Messaouda, from the time of Abd al-Qadir; Kahina, the ancestral queen-mother of the Berbers; and Djamila, too, from the Battle of Algiers. But the heroines of the stories themselves are the generations of women of modern Algeria. Her critique is thus addressed not only to the former occupiers of Algeria but also to those responsible for the present condition of the Algerian woman, often referred to as the second of "two colonialisms." "That look was thought for a long time to be a stolen one because it was that of the stranger, from outside the home and the city. For several decades now, as one nationalism after another is successful, one realizes that inside that Orient delivered unto itself, the image of the woman is no differently perceived: by the father, the husband, and in a way more troubling still, by the brother and the son."[38]

Until now, there have been two spectators, French and Algerian, involved in the observations of and on these postcards; a third spectator is introduced with the English translation of Malek Alloula's study. American readers of *The Colonial Harem*, whether photographers, historians of colonialism, feminist theorists, or literary critics, bring to the photographs another *socius*, other conditions of observation. These are not directly involved perhaps in the French-Algerian controversy, but they are complicit nonetheless in the global politics of history and literature and in the regional distribution of power which is the context of these picture postcards. In other words, according to the perspective of the Moroccan critic Abdelkebir Khatibi:

From the point of view of what is still called the Third World, we cannot pretend that decolonization has succeeded in promoting a radically critical mode of thinking with regard to the ideological machine of imperialism and ethnocentrism, a decolonization which would be at the same time a deconstruction of those discourses which participate in various, more or less dissimulated, ways in imperial domination, understood here also as the power of the word [parole]. No, we have not yet reached that decolonization of thought which would be, over and above a reversal of that power, the affirmation of a difference, and free and absolute subversion of the spirit. There is there something like a void, a silent interval between the fact of colonization and that of decolonization. Not that, here and there, there aren't subversive and responsible words which break forth and are elaborated, but something choked and almost lost remains unspoken, does not assume the power and the risk.[39]

Khatibi goes on to propose a double task for the Arab world, namely, the deconstruction of logo- and ethnocentrism, accompanied by the critique of self-reflexive discourses elaborated by the different Arab societies. Malek Alloula's *The Colonial Harem* rings a like challenge to Western readers and critics.

B.H.

The Colonial Harem

Chapter 1

The Orient as Stereotype and Phantasm

Arrayed in the brilliant colors of exoticism and exuding a full-blown yet uncertain sensuality, the Orient, where unfathomable mysteries dwell and cruel and barbaric scenes are staged, has fascinated and disturbed Europe for a long time. It has been its glittering imaginary but also its mirage.

Orientalism, both pictorial and literary,[1] has made its contribution to the definition of the variegated elements of the sweet dream in which the West has been wallowing for more than four centuries. It has set the stage for the deployment of phantasms.[2]

There is no phantasm, though, without sex, and in this Orientalism, a confection of the best and of the worst—mostly the worst—a central figure emerges, the very embodiment of the obsession: the harem.[3] A simple allusion to it is enough to open wide the floodgate of hallucination just as it is about to run dry.

For the Orient is no longer the dreamland. Since the middle of the nineteenth century, it has inched closer. Colonialism makes a grab for it, appropriates it by dint of war, binds it hand and foot with myriad bonds of exploitation, and hands it over to the devouring appetite of the great mother countries, ever hungry for raw materials.

Armies, among them the one that landed one fine 5 July 1830 a little to the east of Algiers, bring missionaries and scholars with their impedimenta as well as painters and photographers forever thirsty for exoticism, folklore, Orientalism. This fine company scatters all over the land, sets up camp around military messes, takes part in punitive expeditions (even Théophile Gautier is not exempt), and dreams of the Orient, its delights and its beauties.

What does it matter if the colonized Orient, the Algeria of the turn of the century, gives more than a glimpse of the other side of its scenery, as long as the phantasm of the harem persists, especially since it has become profitable? Orientalism leads to riches and respectability. Horace Vernet, whom Baudelaire justly called the Raphael of barracks and bivouacs, is the peerless exponent of this smug philistinism. He spawns imitators. Vulgarities and stereotypes draw upon the entire heritage of the older, precolonial Orientalism. They reveal all its presuppositions to the point of caricature.

It matters little if Orientalistic painting begins to run out of wind or falls into mediocrity. Photography steps in to take up the slack and reactivates the phantasm at its lowest level. The postcard does it one better; it becomes the poor man's phantasm: for a few pennies, display racks full of dreams. The postcard is everywhere, covering all the colonial space, immediately available to the tourist, the soldier, the colonist. It is at once their poetry and their glory captured for the ages; it is also their pseudoknowledge of the colony. It produces stereotypes in the manner of great seabirds producing guano. It is the fertilizer of the colonial vision.

The postcard is ubiquitous. It can be found not only at the scene of the crime it perpetrates but at a far remove as well. Travel is the essence of the postcard, and expedition is its mode. It is the fragmentary return to the mother country. It straddles two spaces: the one it represents and the one it will reach. It marks out the peregrinations of the tourist, the successive postings of the soldier, the territorial spread of the colonist. It sublimates the spirit of the stopover and the sense of place; it is an act of unrelenting aggression against sedentariness. In the post-

card, there is the suggestion of a complete metaphysics of uprootedness.

It is also a seductive appeal to the spirit of adventure and pioneering. In short, the postcard would be a resounding defense of the colonial spirit in picture form. It is the comic strip of colonial morality.

But it is not merely that; it is more. It is the propagation of the phantasm of the harem by means of photography. It is the degraded, and degrading, revival of this phantasm.

The question arises, then, how are we to read today these postcards that have superimposed their grimacing mask upon the face of the colony and grown like a chancre or a horrible leprosy?

Today, nostalgic wonderment and tearful archeology (Oh! those colonial days!) are very much in vogue. But to give in to them is to forget a little too quickly the motivations and the effects of this vast operation of systematic distortion. It is also to lay the groundwork for its return in a new guise: a racism and a xenophobia titillated by the nostalgia of the colonial empire.[4]

Beyond such barely veiled apologias that hide behind aesthetic rationalizations, another reading is possible: a symptomatic one.

To map out, from under the plethora of images, the obsessive scheme that regulates the totality of the output of this enterprise and endows it with meaning is to force the postcard to reveal what it holds back (the ideology of colonialism) and to expose what is repressed in it (the sexual phantasm).

The Golden Age of the colonial postcard lies between 1900 and 1930.[5] Although a latecomer to colonial apologetics, it will quickly make up for its belatedness and come to occupy a privileged place, which it owes to the infatuation it elicits, in the preparations for the centennial of the conquest, the apotheosis of the imperial epoch.

In this large inventory of images that History sweeps with broad strokes out of its way, and which shrewd merchants hoard for future collectors, one theme especially seems to have found favor with the photographers and to have been accorded privileged treatment: the *algérienne*.[6]

History knows of no other society in which women have been photographed on such a large scale to be delivered to public view. This disturbing and paradoxical fact is problematic far beyond the capacity of rationalizations that impute its occurrence to ethnographic attempts at a census and visual documentation of human types.[7]

Behind this image of Algerian women, probably reproduced in the millions, there is visible the broad outline of one of the figures of the colonial perception of the native. This figure can be essentially defined as the practice of a right of (over)sight that the colonizer arrogates to himself and that is the bearer of multiform violence. The postcard fully partakes in such violence; it extends its effects; it is its accomplished expression, no less efficient for being symbolic.[8]

Moreover, its fixation upon the woman's body leads the postcard to paint this body up, ready it, and eroticize it in order to offer it up to any and all comers from a clientele moved by the unambiguous desire of possession.

To track, then, through the colonial representations of Algerian women—the figures of a phantasm—is to attempt a double operation: first, to uncover the nature and the meaning of the colonialist gaze; then, to subvert the stereotype that is so tenaciously attached to the bodies of women.

A reading of the sort that I propose to undertake would be entirely superfluous if there existed photographic traces of the gaze of the colonized upon the colonizer. In their absence, that is, in the absence of a confrontation of opposed gazes, I attempt here, lagging far behind History, to return this immense postcard to its sender.

What I read on these cards does not leave me indifferent. It demonstrates to me, were that still necessary, the desolate poverty of a gaze that I myself, as an Algerian, must have been the object of at some moment in my personal history. Among us, we believe in the nefarious effects of the evil eye (the evil gaze). We conjure them with our hand spread out like a fan. I close my hand back upon a pen to write *my* exorcism: *this text*.

Chapter 2

Women from the Outside: Obstacle and Transparency

The reading of public photographs is always, at bottom, a private reading.
Roland Barthes, *Camera Lucida*

The first thing the foreign eye catches about Algerian women is that they are concealed from sight.

No doubt this very obstacle to sight is a powerful prod to the photographer operating in urban environments.[9] It also determines the obstinacy of the camera operator to force that which disappoints him by its escape.

The Algerian woman does not conceal herself, does not play at concealing herself. But the eye cannot catch hold of her. The opaque veil that covers her intimates clearly and simply to the photographer a refusal. Turned back upon himself, upon his own impotence in the situation, the photographer undergoes an *initial experience of disappointment and rejection*. Draped in the veil that cloaks her to her ankles, the Algerian woman discourages the *scopic desire* (the voyeurism) of the photographer. She is the concrete negation of this desire and thus brings to the photographer confirmation of a triple rejection: the rejection of his desire, of the practice of his "art," and of his place in a milieu that is not his own.

Algerian society, particularly the world of women, is forever forbidden to him. It counterposes to him a smooth and homogenous surface free of any cracks through which he could slip his indiscreet lens.

The whiteness of the veil becomes the symbolic equivalent of blindness: a leukoma, a white speck on the eye of the photographer and on his viewfinder. *Whiteness is the absence of a photo, a veiled photograph, a whiteout, in technical terms.* From its background nothing emerges except some vague contours, anonymous in their repeated resemblance. Nothing distinguishes one veiled woman from another.

Scenes and types. Moorish women taking a walk.

140 ALGER. — Mauresques se rendant au Cimetière. — LL.

L. Rélin, Alger.

5c POSTES

Algiers. Moorish women on their way to the cemetery.

373 ALGER. - *Mauresques en Promenade.* - LL

Algiers. Moorish women taking a walk.

The veil of Algerian women is also seen by the photographer as a sort of perfect and generalized mask. It is not worn for special occasions. It belongs to the everyday, like a uniform. It instills uniformity, the modality of the impossibility of photography, its disappointment and deficiency of expression.

It will be noted that whenever a photographer aims his camera at a veiled woman, he cannot help but include in his visual field several instances of her. As if to photograph one of them from the outside required the inclusion of a *principle of duplication* in the framing. For it is always a group of veiled women that the photographer affixes upon his plate.

One may well wonder about this peculiarity since it could easily be overcome by technical means through the isolation and the enlargement of a detail. This everyday technique of printmaking is never used, however. Does this indicate, perhaps, that the photographer's frustration is generalized and not amenable to being directed toward one individual in the group? Does this mean that his frustration is an induced effect? The society he observes reveals to him the instinctual nature of his desire (voyeurism) and challenges him beyond the defenses of his professional alibi. The exoticism that he thought he could handle without any problems suddenly discloses to him a truth unbearable for the further exercise of his craft.

Moorish women in town attire.

171 *Mauresques se rendent au marabout* J. GEISER - ALGER

Moorish women on their way to a marabout.

Here there is a sort of ironic paradox: the veiled subject—in this instance, the Algerian woman—becomes the purport of an unveiling.

But the veil has another function: to recall, in individualized fashion, the closure of private space. It signifies an injunction of no trespassing upon this space, and it extends it to another space, the one in which the photographer is to be found: public space.

These white islets that dot the landscape are indeed aggregates of prohibition, mobile extensions of an imaginary harem whose inviolability haunts the photographer-voyeur. They are scandalous, or at least perceived as being so. By their omnipresence, they revive frustration. They also recall the existence of the well-known pseudoreligious taboo of the Muslims: the figural depiction of the human body prohibited by Islam.

19. ALGÉRIE
Mauresque - Costume de Ville

Algeria. Moorish woman in city attire.

63 **Mauresque en** promenade *J. Geiser, phot., Alger.*

Moorish woman taking a walk.

These veiled women are not only an embarrassing enigma to the photographer but an outright attack upon him. It must be believed that the feminine gaze that filters through the veil is a gaze of a particular kind: concentrated by the tiny orifice for the eye, this womanly gaze is a little like the eye of a camera, like the photographic lens that takes aim at everything.

The photographer makes no mistake about it: he knows this gaze well; it resembles his own when it is extended by the dark chamber or the viewfinder. Thrust in the presence of a veiled woman, the photographer feels photographed; having himself become an object-to-be-seen, he loses initiative: *he is dispossessed of his own gaze*.

This varied experience of frustration is turned by the photographer into the sign of his own negation. Algerian society, particularly the feminine world within it, threatens him in his being and *prevents him from accomplishing himself as gazing gaze*.

The photographer will respond to this quiet and almost natural challenge by means of a double violation: he will unveil the veiled and give figural representation to the forbidden. This is the summary of his only program or, rather, his symbolic revenge upon a society that continues to deny him any access and questions the legitimacy of his desire. The photographer's studio will become, then, a pacified microcosm where his desire, his scopic instinct, can find satisfaction.

14

And so, now in the studio, adorned for the occasion, is one of the numerous models whom the photographer will have wear the veil (p. 15). As if it were at once part of an exorcism or an act of propitiation, she is drawing the veil aside with both hands in a gesture of inaugural invitation that the photographer has staged (richness of dress, jewelry, smile, etc.), first for himself, and second for the viewer. Separated from the group that rendered her nondescript, the model is holding a pose, haloed in artistic soft focus, the metaphorical equivalent of intense exultation.

This is a determinant moment for what follows because this is where the machinery, or rather the machination, is set in motion. The entire distorting enterprise of the postcard is given here in schematic form. It is contained in the gesture of drawing the veil aside — a gesture executed at the photographer's command and destined to be followed by others. When she completes them, the *algérienne* will no longer have anything to hide.

221 A *Femme Kabyle se couvrant de son Haïck* *ND Phot*

Kabyl woman covering herself with the haik.

15

Chapter 3

Women's Prisons

> At this point, the harem must no longer be considered as some exotic curiosity but must be recognized as a phantasmic locus the fascinating powers of which can be apprehended only if it is related to its deep, metaphysical, roots.
>
> Alain Grosrichard, *Structure du sérail*

The photographer will come up with more complacent counterparts to these inaccessible Algerian women. These counterparts will be paid models that he will recruit almost exclusively on the margins of a society in which loss of social position, in the wake of the conquest and the subsequent overturning of traditional structures, affects men as well as women (invariably propelling the latter toward prostitution).

Dressed for the occasion in full regalia, down to the jewels that are the indispensable finishing touch of the production, the model will manage, thanks to the art of illusion that is photography, to impersonate, to the point of believability, the unapproachable referent: the *other* Algerian woman, absent in the photo. In her semblance on the postcard, the model is simultaneously the epiphany of this absent woman and her imaginary takeover. The perfection and the credibility of the illusion are ensured by the fact that the absent other is, by definition, unavailable and cannot issue a challenge.

Since it fills this absence and this silence, the postcard sets its own criteria of truthfulness for the representation of Algerian women and for the discourse that can be held about them.[10]

Even more advantageously, the existence and the efficacy of the model allow the postcard to conceal the essentially mercantilistic character of its enterprise. For indeed, it must be admitted that the lucrative end of the operation is never apparent on the mercenary bodies displayed on the postcards. It is hidden in at least three ways. First and foremost, by the iconic message, that is, by the photographed subject as such, who must be acknowledged to possess an undeniable power of attraction (one always selects one postcard in preference to another). Second, by the caption, which is meant to be informative; the information it conveys is supposed to amount to "knowledge" and thus be disinterested. Finally, it may occasionally be hidden by the senders' comments with their pretensions to enlightened views.

In her role as substitute, the model presents three distinct and yet closely related advantages: she is *accessible, credible,*[11] and *profitable*. This is the three-legged foundation upon which will come to stand the whole of the enterprise pursued so relentlessly by the colonial postcard.

As the locus for the setting of the illusion, the studio, for its part, must complete the initial illusion created by the model. By virtue of this function, it becomes the scene of the imaginary, indispensable to the fulfillment of desire.[12] It becomes the embodiment of the propitious site.

The whole array of props, carefully disposed by the photographer around and upon the model (trompe l'oeil, furnishings, backdrops, jewelry, assorted objects), is meant to suggest the existence of a natural frame whose feigned "realism" is expected to provide a supplementary, yet by no means superfluous, touch of authenticity. For the mode of being of this counterfeit is redundancy.

Indeed, if the double, or rather the stand-in, is always an impoverished version of the original—its schematic representation—it is because it saturates the meaning of the original by the plethoric multiplication of signs that are intended to connote it. Paradoxically, this would constitute an instance of degradation through excess. The photographer, caught up in his own frenzy, however, cannot stop to consider this paradox, busy as he is with attempting to make something more real than the real and developing an almost obsessive fetishism of the (sign's) object.

S. 2 - N° 11 — MAURESQUE CHEZ ELLE

Moorish women at home.

S. 2 - Nᵒ 12 - ALGÉRIE - MAURESQUES CHEZ ELLES

Moorish women at home.

Brimming over with connotative signs, every photographer's studio thus becomes a versatile segment of urban or geographic landscape. Whereas the model is a figure of the symbolic appropriation of the body (of the Algerian woman), the studio is a figure of the symbolic appropriation of space. They are of a piece together.[13] This double movement of appropriation is nothing more than the expression of the violence conveyed by the colonial postcard, a violence that it speaks of in all innocence, yet cynically.

But beyond such larger considerations, there remains the ineluctable fact that the intromission of model and studio constitutes, for the photographer, the only *technically adequate* means of response to ensure the "survival" of his desire, which means that a structure of substitution is set in place in such a way that it gives the phantasmic faculty access to "reality," albeit an ersatz reality.

In this manner, the theme of the *woman imprisoned in her own home* will impose itself in the most "natural" fashion: by the conjoined play of reverse logic and metaphorical contamination, both determined by the initial frustration.

If the women are inaccessible to sight (that is, veiled), it is because they are imprisoned. This dramatized equivalence between the veiling and the imprisonment is necessary for the construction of an *imaginary scenario* that results in the dissolution of the actual society, the one that causes the frustration, in favor of a phantasm: that of the harem.

The postcard will undertake to display the figures of this phantasm one by one and thus give the photographer the means of a self-accomplishment that he cannot forgo.

Young, then older, girls, and finally women will be made to pose behind bars, their gaze resolutely turned toward this other gaze that looks at them and may bear witness to their confinement. The pose is conventional, hackneyed, and the decor is limited to the obvious signs of incarceration, namely a crisscross of metal bars firmly embedded in wall casings.

SCÈNES et TYPES. — „Aïcha et Zorah"

Scenes and types. "Aicha and Zorah."

Scenes and types. Moorish woman.

Young Moorish woman.

But, in barely perceptible fashion, the meaning of this imprisonment will lose its fixedness and progressively glide toward an even more explicit expression of the sexual nature of the phantasm.

For indeed, these women are first going to be stripped of their clothing by the photographer, in an effort to render their bodies erotic. These bodies may be out of reach, but their very remoteness reveals the voyeurism of the camera operator. This supplemental connotation allows us to consider the colonial post-card, in its "eroticized" form, as the *mise-en-scène* by the photographer of his own voyeurism. To ignore this aspect, this index of obsessiveness, is to risk endowing the colonial postcard with a meaning that was never its own, except in masked form.

One of the cards provides dramatic illustration of the sexual connotation of confinement that is overdetermined by the phantasm of the harem. In it, the imprisonment of women becomes the *equivalent of sexual frustration.* On the other side of the wall, a man is desperately clutching the bars that keep him from the object of his unequivocal yearning. The grimacelike countenance of his face, the mask of suffering that is imprinted on it, leave no doubt about his intention to be united with the prisoner, the woman in the harem.

247 A *Mauresque* ND Phot

Moorish woman.

Types Algériens. — Femme Mauresque. — ND Phot

Algerian types. Moorish woman. (Written on card: I am sending you a package to be picked up at the railway station. The babies are doing well; they have just taken a walk by the beach. I shall write you shortly at greater length. Warm kisses to all of you. [signed:] Martha.)

This ''elaborated'' staging (the tell-taleness of the postcard), which presupposes that the photographer is inside the place of confinement, is highly revealing. *It is the imaginary resolution of the hiatus that differentiates the inside from the outside*; these two spatial categories are perceived as the respective loci of the fulfillment and nonfulfillment of sexual desire. It is also, for the photographer who must have gained access to the female world on the other side of the bars, that is, must have penetrated the harem, the most powerful expression of the symbolic overcoming of the obstacle.

In the paltry space of its representation, the postcard at long last offers the photographer the possibility of roaming through the site of his phantasms, and it melts away the anxiety that attends the inability to achieve self-realization.

Chapter 4

Women's Quarters

It is not impossible to perceive the photographic signifier . . . but it requires a secondary action of knowledge or of reflection.

Roland Barthes, *Camera Lucida*

How is this "secondary act of knowing or of reflection" that Barthes describes to be performed with respect to the colonial postcard if not by acknowledging, from the outset, that the latter is characterized by its extreme mobility as well as by its dubious and devious nature?

Falsely naive, the postcard misleads in direct measure to the fact that it presents itself as having neither depth nor aesthetic pretensions. *It is the "degree zero" of photography*.[14] Common usage acknowledges this proclaimed "modesty": to say of a photograph that it is like a postcard is, by contrast, to grant the good photograph (which a postcard is not) qualities such as depth, expressivity, and aesthetic dimension.

What has rarely been perceived, however, is that the negative qualities (banality, platitude, lack of expressivity, etc.) generally attributed to postcards, and obviously proper to them, are the foundation of an *aesthetics* in the philosophical sense of the term. This aesthetics has the advantage of forcing reflection from the unexpected and inopportune return of criteria applicable to photography. Such a return is a source of constant temptation to the analyst because of the similarity of the two species.

Thus, beyond what is immediately noticeable, the colonial postcard delimits a field distinct from that of photography. And the distinction is not overcome through the opposition of public use versus private use, which is constitutive of it with respect to its specific destination.

The colonial postcard puts into play different motivations, different incentives, that it conceals even more easily because the innocuousness of its facade is granted once for all. Proceeding under the cover of a mask, and setting its meaning into play at several levels, it suggests a sort of resistance by the constant reference to its referent. The postcard, like the photographer in this respect, "has something tautological about it: [in it] a pipe . . . is always and intractably a pipe" (Barthes, *Camera Lucida*, p. 5). Because it has erased the traces, and above all the direction, of its *mise-en-scène*, the colonial postcard can successfully keep up this mirror trick (tautology), so that it presents itself as pure reflection, something it definitely is not.

And so, to take the staging of the *mise-en-scène* apart is to uncover the original triad constituted by the photographer, his model, and his studio. It is to catch them unaware at work on the near side of the referent, that is, before the advent of reflection.

The preceding series of postcards —the imprisoned women—occasionally does let through, albeit in most clumsy fashion, something of the photographer's sexual phantasm, not as the phantasm of an individual, for that would be only of anecdotal interest, but as a *collective phantasm*, proper to colonialism and produced by it.

There would appear to be a contradiction, a breach, here, since the colonial postcard is meant, by definition, *to limit itself to a photographic survey of society and landscape*. That at least is its ethnographic alibi, its avowed purpose. But rather than a contradiction, in the case of the colonial postcard, it would be better to speak of a specific mode of operation that consists in the maintenance, though in constant scramble (the ruse), of a triple agency: that of the *avowal* (ethnography), that of the *unsaid* (colonial ideology), and that of the *repressed* (phantasm).

Proceeding in this manner, the colonial postcard will set up a *rhetoric of camouflage* in which only the agency of avowal will appear in the forefront, no matter what theme the photographer may select. Paradoxically, this omnipresence of avowal brings to mind the behavior patterns of disavowal, and it is well known what *they* signify. The captions of the postcard make this *disavowal* explicit. A photograph of a woman with her breasts bare calls forth the mind-boggling truism: "Moorish woman" or "Young Moorish woman" (pp. 24 and 26).

The reader may object, and with reason, that this is an extreme case and therefore one of rather disarming naiveté. Indeed, *all* of the avowal is not to be found in the captions.

The colonial postcard is inseparable from that which occasioned its existence, and therefore it offers to partake in the vast project of exploring the colony. Thus, taking its place among specialized monographs on defined topics, it proposes an approach that is more intimate and more directly visual. In addition, because of its accessibility in the colonial world, it assumes the guise of an illustrated popular encyclopedia. This is one of the reasons why it follows the "progress" of colonization and why its Golden Age is between 1900 and 1930. The exotic postcard is the vulgar expression of colonial euphoria just as much as Orientalist painting was, in its beginnings, the Romantic expression of the same euphoria.

On the other hand, since it is now its own self-justification, the postcard is freed from the need to put itself in question by the telltale existence it leads. Its "realistic" underlay, indispensable to its continued upkeep and uttering of the avowal, allows it to obstruct the horizon of its productions, all of which are meant to convey a "truth" upon the colony.

When it is transposed into the world of women, this avowal (the ethnographic aim) must presuppose, to remain credible, an intimacy that was gained in, and over, the observed society, a total transparence, already established in the previous series of cards although in imperfect manner since the repressed manifested its return in the guise of exposed women.[15]

But no matter, the avowal cannot be stopped by such lapses without running the risk of coming to a premature end and thus revealing its falsehood, its duplicity.

Moorish woman.

6240 SCÈNES ET TYPES. — *Groupe de Mauresques.* — LL.

Scenes and types. Group of Moorish women.

Scenes and types. Moorish women of Algiers. (Written on card: Anatoly's woman, R[. . .]'s woman.)

Algeria. Group of Moorish women. (Written on card: Don't get bored [signed:] L. Maurice.)

461 Mauresques dans leur intérieur.   *J. Geiser, phot.-Alger.*

Moorish women in their quarters.

144. ALGÉRIE — Belle Fatma

Algeria. Beautiful Fatmah.

The women's quarters that the postcard sets out to explore cannot sustain the illusion after a while, however, even though the ethnographic alibi seems to suit it perfectly.

Again, the model and the studio will greatly compensate for the weakness of the theme and the poverty of the imagination.

A few young women, seated on mats, posing in front of a hanging carpet will suffice to suggest the familiarity of the photographer with the inside of this female world. The forced smile is there to further emphasize the illusory complicity that the photographer steals from his models.

The postcards that exhibit this theme speak for themselves: for example, the squatting woman whose expression is the epitome of boredom while her companions stand forever at attention. It is easy to imagine the photographer moving among the models, issuing instructions on posture, and generally improving the group's photographic appearance, which, incidentally, calls to mind the passing in review of the troops so dear to colonial sensibilities.

Besides the obvious fact of their fabrication, these photos bring forth an illusion, the first victim of which is the photographer,[16] who is content to be taken in. Like a new Alice, the camera operator has gone through the looking glass. But what he discovers, upon landing at the end of his leap, is only the reflection that he elicits himself and elaborates. What he brings back from his expedition is but a harvest of stereotypes that express both the limits of fabricated realism and those of models frozen in the hicratic poses of death.

To photograph these women in "their" quarters, "their" interior, is tantamount for the photographer, however, to have come, on discrete tippy toes, close to a highly eroticized reality of the Oriental world that haunts him: the harem. A lascivious world of idle women that lie adorned as if ready for unending festivities, the harem is deeply fascinating and equally disturbing. No doubt the conjunction of both of these responses is the basis for the photographic success of the postcard on p.33. Having closed in upon something other than the unrelieved and boring expression of a stereotype, the photographer manages to convey a little of his excitement, of his jubilant vacillation.

Is it the aesthetically perfect presence of these ten women, whose gazes converge upon the one who is looking at them, that holds our attention? A sort of calm aura of harmony and equilibrium gives the composition an ambience rarely found elsewhere.[17]

What is also striking about this postcard is no doubt its power of evocation, which turns it into a sort of masterpiece of the genre. When one looks at it, one cannot help but see it as a kind of photographic synthesis of Delacroix's *Women of Algiers* and of Ingres's *Turkish Bath*. Such a "pictorialism," to apply Barthes's formula (*Camera Lucida*, p. 31), "is only an exaggeration of what the Photograph thinks of itself."

For the colonial postcard, whose daily lot is the stereotype, this exaggeration turns to madness, harem madness.

Moorish women in their quarters.

Chapter 5

Couples

Photography is worse than eloquence: it asserts that nothing is beyond penetration, nothing is beyond confusion, and that nothing is veiled.

Paul Morand, *Le Réveille-Matin* (1937)

We know henceforth that the photographer has adequate means at his disposal to deal with any subject, in his own way of course. One such subject is couples, and it presents a compelling ethnographic interest. As the constitutive unit of society, the couple cannot be photographically avoided.

However, in contrast to the series on "women's quarters" in which the documentation is relatively large, the series on couples turns out to be quite lean. The nature of the subject as well as the difficulty of finding male models no doubt explains this shortcoming of photographic "inspiration," this thematic gap.

Moreover, if it is true that Algerian society is generally loath to let itself be photographed, it makes sense that it would be, *a fortiori*, even more loath to do so in the case of couples. The mixing of the sexes that is presupposed by photographing a couple is doubly inconceivable in the Algerian family at the beginning of the century.

But none of that can dissuade the photographer from his undertaking. The Algerian couple is just as counterfeitable as the rest of his subjects for the sake of the cause. And so the photographer carries out, around this new theme, a procedure that could already be seen at work in what has preceded and which once again makes apparent the consequences of the distortion introduced by staging the photograph.[18]

A society in which social space is strictly divided into an inside and an outside cannot possibly accommodate a gaze that, by definition, abolishes this rigid partition and seeks to make public that which is concealing itself. The photog-

Algeria. Native family.

rapher's gaze reflects his dream of total transparency, of an absence of shadows, of a world in which uninterrupted communication would reign between two mutually exclusive spaces.

When it undertakes to represent the couple, the postcard does much more than it intends: *it juxtaposes two perfectly heterogeneous spaces without any regard for a social equilibrium that it can neither understand nor accept.* The artificiality of the pose, which upsets the established order (and the partition of space is part of this order), is visible in the self-concious and assumed attitudes of the models supposed to reconstitute couples in front of the lens. This suggests that such an order, which the models must have interiorized since they are part of Algerian society, sets up resistances that are not very easy to overcome even under conditions of simulation.

The very idea of the couple is an imported one which is applied to a society that operates on the basis of formations that are greater than simple twoness, such as the extended family, the clan, or the tribe. The couple, in the Western sense, is an aberration, a historical error, an unthinkable possibility in Algerian society.

Beyond a simple photographic act that, in a sense, would either proclaim its innocence or assert its commonplace, the representation of the couple is the expression of a double symbolic violence perpetrated upon Algerian society: it rearranges its space and its structure on the basis of alien criteria.

We have here the implementation of an arbitrariness that precedes the postcard and provides it with its "moral" justification: colonial arbitrariness. For its part, the colonial postcard offers to this original arbitrariness—which it obviously does not see in these terms—an expression that is perniciously idealized because it presents it as "objectively" accomplished (the credit of photographic evidence), of one of the chief objectives of colonization, namely the breakup of the very kernel of the resistance to colonial penetration: the traditional family.

First colonized, then rearranged along bourgeois criteria, the Algerian family becomes, in the postcard, only the exotic (see the dress) replica of its European counterpart.

In the imaginary space of the postcard, where all social connections have been reduced and put out of sight, the ideal social unit in which the modern couple, itself the expression of a more rational order of which colonization is supposedly the purport, finally makes its appearance and takes the place of the "anarchic," irreducible, traditional family.

6282 SCÈNES ET TYPES. — *Famille Mauresque.* — LL.

Scenes and types. Moorish family.

The photographer makes these couples posing in the studio express more than they are capable of saying. He *manipulates*, in spite of them (note the stiff and reticent attitudes), a meaning of which their bodies (forced to stand side by side in the representation of the couple) are the silent yet eloquent signs. There is also evident here another aspect of the symbolic violence, but this time it is carried out upon individuals who are made exemplary by the postcard. The photographer frees himself of the responsibility for this violence by the remuneration given to the model, thus acquitting himself of the violation that he secretly perpetrates.

If one examines these photographic documents a little more closely, another objective becomes apparent beyond the ethnographic concern of the photographers. He has taken care to preserve the everyday appearance of the couples that are immortalized in them: they wear ordinary clothing. This forced "realism" is supposed to suggest a scene taken from life, a snapshot, that is, to guarantee additional truthfulness, something that the postcard is particularly eager to have since that is what it most lacks.[19]

These photos of couples have another characteristic linked to their preoccupation with realism: children appear alongside their fictional parents.

This addition of children answers to another necessity as well, less easy to acknowledge than the idyllic portrait of the family. It aims to evoke the idea of a birthrate perceived as being out of control, which colonial ideology attributes to "cultural belatedness" and to stagnation. It suggests the swarming of an anarchic progeny that certainly received its share of critical attention in colonial literature, where it was denounced as a sequela to the state of barbarism that preceded colonization. The postcard takes over this bromide in order to illustrate it in its own way, that is, by making it visual.

From this perspective, the postcard on p. 42 is of a rare eloquence since it presents, against the backdrop of a natural decor, a couple with a child, in which the spouses are no more than twelve or thirteen years old. The very possibility of such a falsification tells us a great deal about the permanence of the great colonialist stereotypes and about their almost obsessive character. What this document insists upon, beyond any possibility of verisimilitude, is the idea of a monstrous barbarism that does not even spare childhood.

To the innocent games of adolescence, barbarism substitutes the weight of premature paternity and maternity. Young girls do not play with dolls but already rock flesh-and-blood babies in their arms—when they are not feeding them from their barely formed breasts.

This "laying waste" of childhood is further aggravated, if that is possible, by the photographer, who adds here and there redundant signs that serve as the

6147 SCÈNES ET TYPES. — *Famille devant leur Maison* — LL

Scenes and types. Family in front of their house.

Scenes and types. Young couple from the South.

Scenes and types. The Lovers.

necessary reminders of backwardness. These include the rags of the ''parents'' and of the ''child''; the trachoma of the ''baby,'' whose head disappears beneath an unspeakable bandage; and generally a repugnant squalor presented as both characteristic and congenital, and staged for the edification of those who persist in refusing to see the humanitarian grandeur of the colonial enterprise.

At a time when mass media do not yet exist, the postcard fills the gap and adds its ''inspired'' chatter to colonialist discourse. Moreover, it provides it with a custom-made iconography, replete with pious and worthy intentions. *It is an illustrated breviary*.

For its part, the postcard on p. 43 contributes to the same end but, this time, in a valorized mode. The couple represented here is in the process of mutating; it is miraculously saved; in other words, it is a couple already visited by the blessings of civilization: it has been the recipient of divine grace. The young horse-guard (or rifleman) in full uniform may indeed hold his companion amorously because he partakes in the colonial order and has thus extricated himself from the ambient barbarism. He stands confident and assured; he smiles at the future. His companion, dressed and adorned as richly as it is possible to be, confirms this irresistible social climb. which is offered here as a dazzling model. The absence of progeny lets us conclude that the postcard depicts a *good management of sexuality*,

one way of reaching the heights promised by civilization.

A comparison of the two postcards on pp. 42 and 43 yields a sort of dream of the colonial ideology that could be formulated as follows: *sterilize and castrate the couple in order to have it conform to the status of a true colonized couple*.

One can see here one of the dreadful apprehensions of any establishment of colonial dominion over alien populations: sooner or later the native birthrate will threaten, with its rapid growth, the future of the colony. The postcard, in addressing this theme, attempts an absurd and imaginary conjuration of the inexorable movement of history, a movement it resolutely ignores in order to concentrate on a present that it is busy counterfeiting.

To the photographer and his clientele at least, the representation of the couple remains a relatively neutral and harmless subject inasmuch as the ethnographic alibi can be invoked to conceal the hidden meaning.

But the postcard is a naive "art" that rests, and operates, upon a false equivalency (namely, that illusion equals reality). *It literally takes its desires for realities*.

Its desires are, first and foremost, those of the photographer, and among them the absolute necessity of the harem as imaginary figure and phantasmic site is well known. And so, it is to be expected that it will manifest itself in this theme as well.

6262   SCÈNES ET TYPES. — *Famille Arabe.* — LL.

Scenes and types. Arab family.

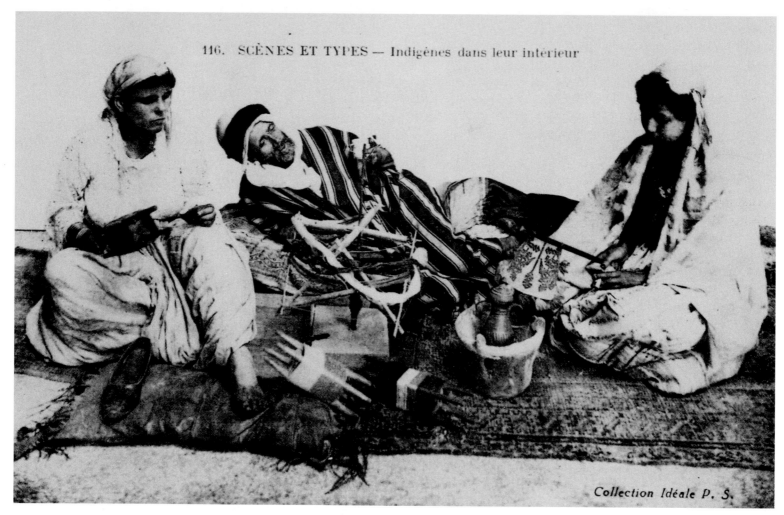

116. SCÈNES ET TYPES — Indigènes dans leur intérieur

Collection Idéale P. S.

Scenes and types. Natives in their quarters.

If the harem suggests the possibility that one man may do as he wishes with several women, it is clear that bigamy is already a harem in rudimentary form, a reduced-scale harem. As soon as the photographer attempts to represent an Algerian man with two wives, without disturbing the family frame of this series of postcards, the obsessing figure of the phantasm begins to hover about.

The image of bigamy is, so to speak, a partial payment on the pleasure that is elicited by the idea of the harem. *Although bigamy does not imply the excesses of sensuality characteristic of life in the harem, it constitutes a compulsory figure of the representation, no doubt necessary to the workings of the colonial dream.*

303. - ALGERIE. - Scènes et types. - Le Five O'Clock Tea

Collection B. B.

Algeria. Scenes and types. Five o'clock tea.

Chapter 6

The Figures of the Harem: Dress and Jewelry

The order of the seraglio is set with the despot in view and according to his needs, and most of all for sexual pleasure which begins with the privilege of sight.

Alain Grosrichard, *Structure du sérail*

With respect to pleasure, the harem cannot be likened to the undifferentiated addition of interchangeable, and therefore perfectly equivalent and anonymous, elements. In this respect, it is the antithesis of repetition. It cannot be a sum of monogamies.

The phantasmic value of the harem is a function of this presumed absence of limitation to a sexual pleasure lived in the mode of frenzy, and which is conceivable only if, in each instance, its object is different, unique, irreplaceable, and perfectly individualized.

A series as abundant as that of the postcards taking dress and jewelry as their theme gives an idea of the imaginary's requirement of renewed difference, or rather of *different repetition*. It is the equivalent, in the order of images, of the compulsive tendency characteristic of *wish fulfillment*. The repetition and the tireless variation of the same pose constitute a sort of *enumeration*: the photographer thus proceeds to a roll call of the inmates of an imaginary harem.

All the women called out one by one, who can only comply with the call (that is what they are paid for), are required by the photographer to dress and adorn themselves as if they were to attend a feast. They are made-up, covered with gold, to be infinitely beautiful and desirable, dreamy and distant, submissive and regal.

It is the nature of pleasure to scrutinize its object detail by detail, to take possession of it in both a total and a fragmented fashion. It is an intoxication, a loss of oneself in the other through sight.

142. ALGÉRIE — Belle Fatma

Pour vous jrouter, monsieur

Algeria. Beautiful Fatmah.

147. ALGÉRIE. — Belle Fatma

Algeria. Beautiful Fatmah.

The voyeurism of the photographer here reaches a rare pinnacle, something that provides the viewer with a remarkable series of portraits that, by their inherent aesthetic quality, keep on renewing the same pleasure: the one that lies at their origin, the frisson of which is carried over from one variation to another. The emotion must have been strong indeed to make possible such an intense jubilation of the gaze. But one begins to sense that, beyond these dazzling figures, there is an anticipation of something else, the paroxysmal occurrence of which is being deferred and suspended.

The "logic" of desire, which I have been reconstructing in these pages, conceals its procedure precisely by that which discloses it. Its meaning is deliberately arrested, frozen upon a surface that misleads the eye through numerous calls for its attention and through unexpected but cleverly utilized distractions. The saturation of the image that is sought by the photographer has no other aim than to lead the eye astray, to set glittering traps for it, and to direct it entirely to that which is offered to view.

Does this mean, then, that this entire deployment is useless because of the very thing that it occults? that the existence of the occulted (phantasm) deprives that which is apparent of reality? Certainly not.

We are apparently touching upon one of the contradictions that arises in the interpretation of the colonial postcard.

Until now we have stressed the relation of the illusion to the reality that it is supposed to reflect. We must now admit that a *kernel of truth*, or rather, of verisimilitude, survives beyond the conventionalism of the pose and of the stereotype.

This exception, much more noticeable here than elsewhere, must be attributed to the nature of the subject. At no time has the camera gotten so close to the model to emphasize her resemblance to the original. We now have something very much akin to a series of closeups on details of dress and ornament. The counterfeit realism of the postcard requires a minimum of truthfulness without which the whole thing would degenerate into gratuitous fantasy. Moreover, this series, by virtue of its profound significance, requires a painstaking attention to details which has intermittently left very clear traces.

This "exactness," which is limited to details, makes possible an enumeration of the different jewels of the dress as well as of the components of traditional garb. The photographer varies the dress and the jewels according to regions.

The apparent aim is to create a sort of *exhaustive, descriptive catalog of the finery* of Algerian women.[20] This series must be seen as the rare success of an enterprise in which the ethnographic alibi *almost* coincides with its tangible results.

69 — LA BELLE "FATMAH" chez elle en costume de gala

Beautiful "Fatmah" at home in full regalia.

390 Belle Fatma

Beautiful Fatmah.

Truthfulness in details may very well not constitute the truthfulness of the whole, however. The elements of dress and the jewels, viewed separately, are factual, but their arrangement on the model fails to produce an impression of veracity. The accumulation of all of these accessories upon a single individual creates a saturated effect that is detrimental to verisimilitude. It looks as if the photographer had at his disposal a large and varied stock of jewelry and apparel and could not stop himself from having the model wear it all at once.

204 Femme Kabyle

J. Geiser, phot.-Alger.

Kabyl woman.

395 Femme du Sud

J. GEISER, PHOT. - ALGER

Woman from the South.

Femme Kabyle

N· 201   Phot. Leroux. Alger   Kabyl woman.

Mauresque chez elle

236

Moorish woman at home.

58

197 A *Femme des Ouled-Naïls*

ND Phot

'Uled-Nayl woman.

'Uled-Nayl woman.

Femme des Ouled-Nails

174 A

N.D. Phot

'Uled-Nayl woman.

154   Jeune Bédouine

J. Geiser, phot.-Alger.

Young Beduin woman.

Bedecked in this manner, decorated so to speak, these Algerian women in full regalia bear some resemblance to the Virgins carried in Spanish processions. And that is indeed the impression they all give: they are ecstatic icons, passively submitting to their cosmetic make-over,[21] readied for the *other scene*, for a feast of the phantasm, whose secret is known only to the photographer. The model and what she signifies (the Algerian woman) are effaced to become no more than the purport of a *carnivalesque orgy*.

This slide toward the improbable, caused by the saturation of the image and well beyond the photographer's control, is evident in the most flagrant way in a set of three documents in which the same model, wearing the same outfit, photographed by the same photographer at the same location, represents in turn a "Young Beduin Woman," a "Young Woman from the South," and a "Young Kabyl Woman" (pp. 62, 63, and 65)! This incoherent and hasty minglement tells us more than anything else about the photographer's presuppositions and how the postcard functions.

Nai Type du [...].

291 Jeune fille du Sud — J. Geiser, phot.-Alger.

Young woman from the South.

For the photographer, the model is essentially a *vagrant and unformed* individual whom he alone can attach to a site (the South, Kabylia, etc.) and endow with identity and status (young Kabyl woman, woman from the South, etc.). Thanks to the postcard, the model traverses Algerian society through and through; at every one of her stops (signified by the pose, the change of decor in the studio, or simply by the caption), she is supposed to reflect a part of reality.

From this point of view, the model is another figure of the obsession to penetrate Algerian society which haunts colonialism. She is also another figure of the desire for transparency. In the model's summary, and representation, of herself, Algerian society ceases to be opaque, in the imaginary at least. That is, it ceases to be stubbornly resistive to the violation that it suffers. *In its illusive dissolution of actual resistance, the colonial postcard offers a view of a pacified reality, restored to the colonial order, which presently proceeds to draw up an inventory of it.*

In addition, the model proves to be so pliable because the "art" of the exotic postcard is an art of sign and not an art of meaning. The few signs distributed here and there over the reflective surface of the postcard (pottery, jewelry, rugs, utensils, garments, etc.) are its true subjects; the rest are nothing more than staging in the best of cases, and masquerade more often than not.

Inherently incapable of avoiding this sham, the colonial postcard proceeds through coarse condensations and clumsy allusions; therein lies its essence.

The reflection of a reflection, the exotic (and/or colonial) postcard is above all an art of simulacrum, in both the theatrical and the compensatory sense of the term.

These *algériennes*, bedecked like revellers, are themselves but simulacra (that is, phantoms), even if some fragments of truth manage to fasten themselves to them and remain afloat in this tidal wave of colonial bad taste.

The commercial success of this simulacrum is not surprising since it is directed to the very people who stand at its inception: soldiers, colonizers, and visitors from the mother country in search of local color.

But the continued success of the simulacrum, through the infinite variation of its figures and its tireless power of attraction to the photographer, is a further indication that, beyond its flagrant sordidness, there are other motivations, of a sexual nature.

381 Jeune fille kabyle

J. Geiser, phot., Alger.

Young Kabyl woman.

93. SCÈNES ET TYPES
Mauresque de Laghouat

Scenes and types. Moorish woman from
Laghuat.

66

Chapter 7

Inside the Harem: The Rituals

The women have no scruples in front of Christian slaves because, they say, they are blind.

Le Chevalier d'Aranda (1671)

By its very nature, photography constantly establishes and maintains a distance. It distances, and it inscribes this gap into its texture. As the imaginary accomplishment of a phantasm, it carries within itself a *principle of deception*. By virtue of this fact, it instigates its infinite return, and, in each instance, it weaves the phantasmic web all over again.

Photography nourishes the voyeurism of the photographer but never satiates it because this voyeurism, as the structure of desire, has neither beginning nor end. It is unformed outside of the instinct that characterizes it. It is therefore an infinite undertaking, having this plethora of images that tirelessly repeat the same subjects: one photographer copying another, and so on.

It is as if all the authors of postcards suffered from the same disease of the inspiration, from the same inability to get off the well-trodden and well-marked paths that force them to circle endlessly, in ways that are most unlikely to give rise to any emotion, around the object of their desire (the Algerian woman through her substitute, the model).

For the situation of the postcard photographer is well-nigh untenable. He is stuck in a dead end in which he has trapped himself. He is a being of desire, the specific originality of everyone of us, but he does not have the means to satisfy this desire.

A closer examination of this photographer's art may well lead us to better delimit the nature and the mode of operation of this principle of deception.

In contrast to the ordinary photographer, the author of postcards, as soon as he takes up a theme like that of Algerian women, deals exclusively with substitutes (the model) and simulacra (the studio and the props disposed around it). This means that he must first compose the photograph that he shoots, and that he must do so *materially* in the studio. He must stage it. In doing so, he literally *decomposes* (deconstructs) the very thing that propels him: his scopic instinct which, by definition, is pure relationality by means of the gaze.

And so his voyeurism, already altered and degraded by the necessary setup he must arrange, is carried out once removed: it encompasses a product that is degraded as well, the copy of a scene that has had no other existence than a made-up one.

With his attachment to his print, the author of postcards is more like an amateur painter searching for exoticism than a photographer.[22]

No doubt the author of postcards has come to terms with the fact that he has to live his phantasm by proxy. And so he delegates to his anonymous and sizable clientele, for whom the postcard is still reality put into images, the task of redeeming him. Ultimately, he will have no other avenue of escape than the pleasure of the other—a pleasure that he will have helped rouse and sustain. His role will not be any different from that of the intermediary, the procurer, who takes pleasure in the pleasure of the other, whom he imagines taking his pleasure. Such an intermediary is thus but a variant of the voyeur.

This reversal, or rather, this derivation, is not surprising or dramatic. It points out only a "natural" tendency that the postcard photographer, like the sorcerer's apprentice, discovers and experiences at his own expense. It also indicates the meaning and the existence of another, and much largre, phantasm: the colonial phantasm, in which the photographer is enmeshed.

The fact that, in spite of its avatars, the phantasm of the harem retains its efficacy upon the photographer is eloquent testimony to its extensive reach. *Affecting the colonial world without being the contrivance of any single individual, this phantasm is the equivalent of a mental habit (mentalité), a "cultural" habitus, characteristic of those to whom an algérienne can only be a "Fatmah" or a "Mouquère"* [23] and definitely a desirable inmate of the harem.

And so, redeemed as far as he is concerned—if he ever felt guilty—the postcard photographer can pursue his laborious but certainly not unprofitable "inquiry."

To see the inside of the harem is to follow its inhabitants as they tend to their various appointed tasks and to turn the representations of these activities into the obvious sign of a familiarity that finally manages to establish itself.

Better yet, to be the witness of such intimacy is to partake in it. And so, magically, the photographer enters through the main door into this holy of holies. He is no longer the surreptitious and sneaky visitor who steals away with a few meager scraps when a favorable occasion arises. Quite the contrary, having lifted the curtain, he roams openly throughout the harem, undisturbed, observing at leisure the life that is hidden from indiscreet eyes.

The harem, though opened up by the photographer, must remain symbolically closed. For the phantasm, a public harem is inconceivable. This apparent contradiction between what the postcard unveils and displays and what desire wants to keep secret is resolved by the photographer through a more elaborate staging. This means that the studio is redecorated with trompe l'oeil or moved to locations that have typical harem "architecture." Both the trompe l'oeil and the natural decor (arcades, colonnades, inner courtyards, etc.) must suggest an inaccessible depth, a mystery beyond what is represented. What the card brings to light, then, may suffice for purposes of jubilation, but it is by no means all. This *all* is, in any case, out of the frame.

589 Femme Arabe dans son Intérieur

Arab woman in her quarters.

Woman from southern Algeria. 92 Femme du Sud Algérien

70

131. ALGÉRIE — Mauresque versant son kaoua

Collection Idéale P. S.

Algeria. Moorish woman pouring her kaoua.

Collection Idéale P. S.

150. SCÈNES ET TYPES — Le Kaoua

Scenes and types. Kaoua.

The photographer carefully orchestrates his effects, so to speak, and the idea of the harem as a labyrinthine space underscores the importance of the backdrop, which consists entirely of a succession of secret alcoves, hidden doors, courtyards leading to more courtyards, and so on. At the same time that it exposes, the postcard opens up an abyssal perspective within itself.

Three figures, minor ones to be sure, especially in the light of what is expected and what must follow, will bear the burden of signifying the new intimacy achieved by the photographer, by virtue of which he finds himself in the center of the privileged locus, both a jubilant guest and a deeply affected witness. These three figures must converge to evoke the idle and voluptuous daily regimen of the harem.

First and foremost comes the coffee ceremony (or *kaoua* as it is called by the white trash of the colony in their emergent pidgin). This subtheme, repeated *ad nauseam*, besides showing women pouring or sipping coffee, at times in startlingly acrobatic postures, is supposed to initiate the viewer into a drinking ceremony the rules and decorum of which are set by the harem. It would appear that coffee, as sign, is endowed with such a rich polysemy that, by itself, it fills in for a number of other signs that are contiguous to it (tea, various sherbets, etc.).

Algiers. Arab women having coffee.

For the photographer as well as for the viewer, kaoua is the sublimation of the aromatic soul of the Orient.

These beautiful women, wholly given to the coffee that they take alone or in a group, are supposed to suggest, by their languor and their unending reverie, a metaphysics of refreshment and odoriferous absorption.

Coffee profiles a *long metaphor of sweetness* (Turkish delights, baklavas, sweet wines, syrupy liquors, ambrosia, and nectar) that rapidly recedes from view because of the lifeless artificiality of the pose and the conventionalism of the decor. Everywhere the same inlaid table is covered with the same copper platter on which stand the same cups that are so awkward to drink from. All this paraphernalia, combined with such an obvious poverty of imagination, turns the metaphor into a schema—worse, a stereotype. But that is the expression of a rather banal and yet deadly fate that is very familiar to the postcard.

Just like the coffee from which it is inseparable, the hookah, the second symbol of the inner harem, repeats with even greater insistence the stereotypical reference to the Orient. It clumsily completes it. There is no Orient without the hookah.

It matters little that it is rarely used in Algeria and that its use has more to do with interior decoration than with instrumental efficacy. What the photograph demands from it and retains is a connotation. As an absolutely necessary prop, the hookah extends the suggestion initiated by the coffee.

The simple evocation of the hookah, associated with hashish, suffices to give life to a world of dreamy feminine presences, in various states of self-abandonment and lasciviousness, welcoming and without reserve. It implies general stupefaction of the senses that foreshadows their unbridled release. The women who smoke the hookah are no longer of this, the observable, world: they move in the ethereal space of the harem.

But here again the postcard faithfully fulfills its reductive role: it wrecks the reverie before it manages to give rise to it. In this flea-market decor, the hookah becomes an embarrassment of serpentine pipes from which the model does not know how to extricate herself. One of the "charms of the Orient" turns into a silent-movie gag.

The odalisque,[24] the third and last figure of the harem's inside, forms a sort of focal point toward which all the scattered references converge in order to be redeployed.

Ideal figure above all others, the odalisque is the very symbol of the harem, its highest expression. She fills it with a presence that is at once mysterious and luminous. She is its hidden, yet available, core, always throbbing with restrained sensuality.

323. ALGÉRIE — Mauresque fumant le Narguileh

Algeria. Moorish woman smoking a hookah.

Arab women.

139. ALGÉRIE. — Meriem fumant le narguileh.

Algeria. Meriem smoking a hookah.

Hiding in the deepest recesses of the harem, where she reclines in lascivious self-abandon, the odalisque has become the goal of the photographer. For this obsessive guest of the harem, she is the very personification of the phantasm, its fermata.

It is unnecessary for the photographer to capture the pleasure that the odalisque evokes. This is a subject with a long pictorial history which advantages him. But what Ingres's Odalisques, for example, express in latent eroticism and sensual presence, the colonial postcard displays boldly, filling in the gaps with all the conventional and redundant implements at its disposal.

And then it begins: one odalisque is lying down with her blouse indecently wide open, exposing alluring breasts that entice the eyes as surely as they cause them to avert their gaze (p. 80). A pornography that does not yet own up to its true nature ostentatiously begins to supplant an eroticism whose only excuse is that it was never there in the first place.

By contrast, it is undoubtedly the absence of any pornographic idea and the play of a pleasing chiaroscuro that turn the last odalisque of the series into a sort of masterpiece. The physical beauty of the model, her dress, her ornaments, as well as the languorous but regal pose—all in the middle ground of the shot—contribute to the creation of an atmosphere of mystery that is sufficiently attractive in itself.

We would have a perfect "pictorialism," one of the ideals that the postcard strives for but never achieves, were it not for the fetishism of the photographer, who trivializes the effect by the inopportune adjunction of a hookah that stands out in the foreground, breaking up the graceful extension of the legs.

This tawdriness that keeps reappearing is beyond the control of the postcard. It is its original sin, its mark of infamy, in sum, its signature at the bottom of a counterfeit.

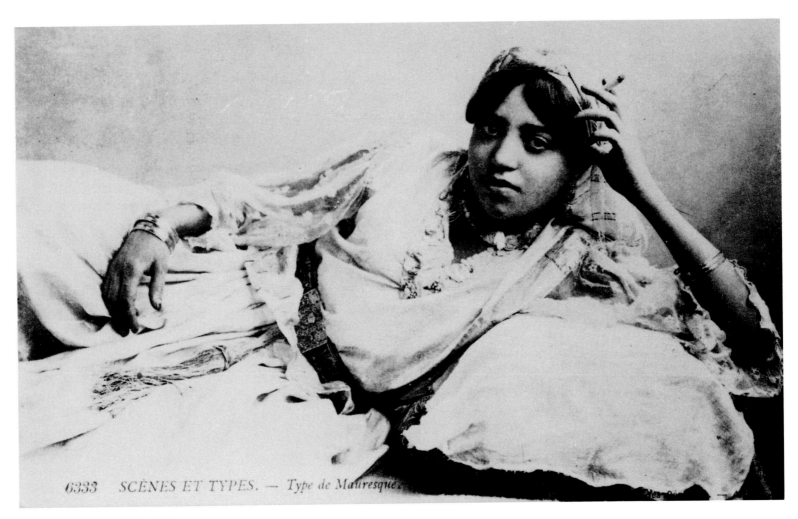

6333 SCÈNES ET TYPES. — Type de Mauresque

Scenes and types. Moorish woman.

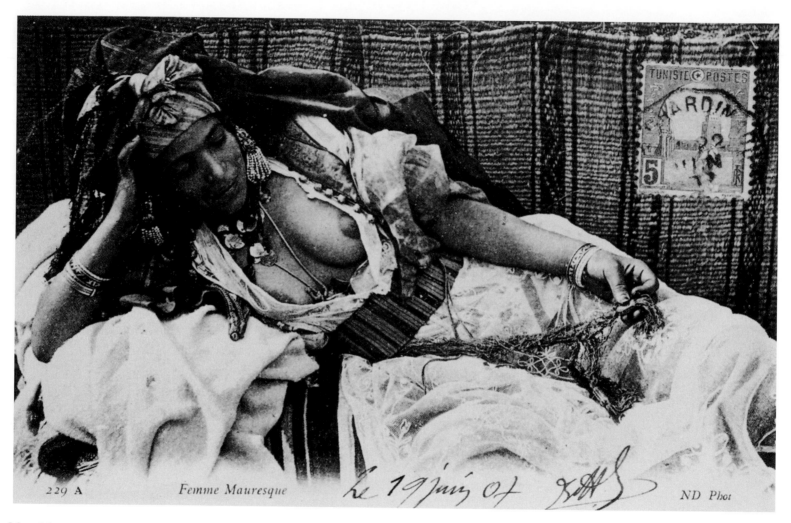

Moorish woman.

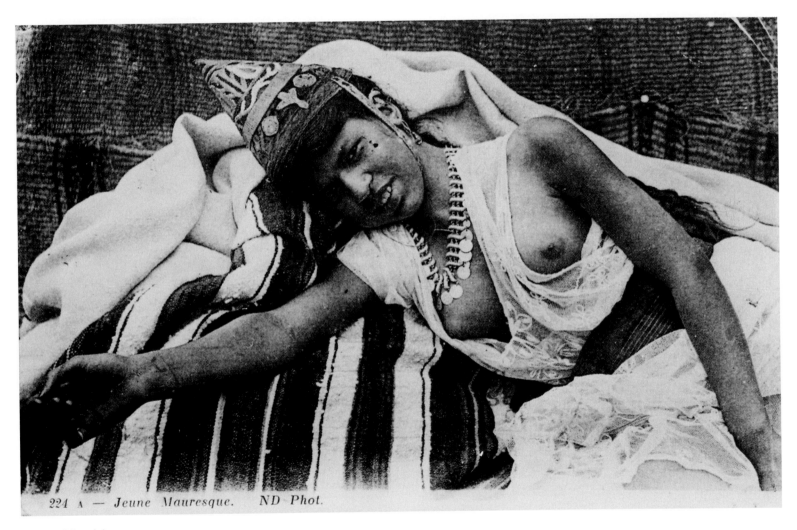

224 A — *Jeune Mauresque.* ND Phot.

Young Moorish woman.

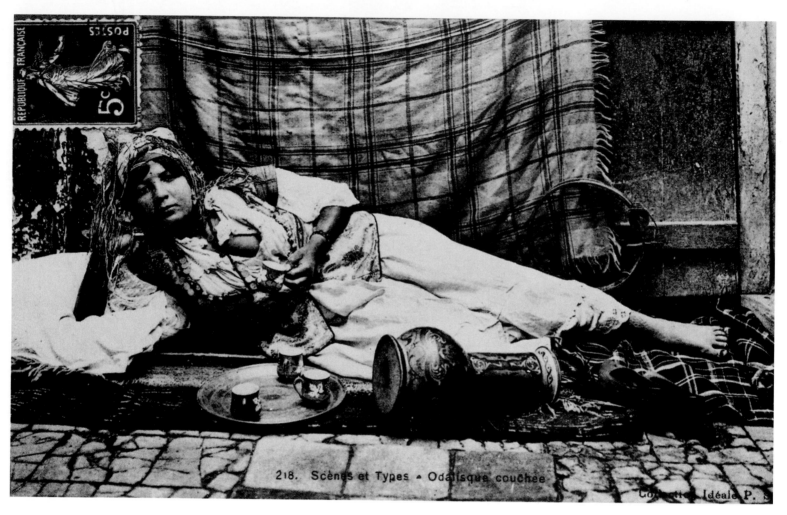

218. Scènes et Types • Odalisque couchée

Scenes and types. Reclining odalisque.

6284   SCÈNES ET TYPES. — *Mauresque dans son Intérieur*. — LL.

Scenes and types. Moorish woman in her quarters.

Chapter 8

Song and Dance: Almehs and Bayaderes

Bayaderes. — All the women of the Orient are bayaderes. This word carries the imagination very far.

Gustave Flaubert, *Dictionary of Received Ideas*

Swinging of the hips, twisting of the body, head jerks and arm developpés, a succession of voluptuous and swooning attitudes, such are the foundations of dance in the Orient.

Théophile Gautier, *Voyage pittoresque en Algérie* (1845)

The three complementary figures discussed in chapter 7 define *the essence of the harem* more than they describe its inner life. No doubt such a "stylization" was made necessary and imposed by a sort of principle of gradation of pleasure. But there are also, and they prove to be determinant, technical limitations inherent in the postcard, which come to further extend the incapacity of the photographer and his want of creativity.

The odalisque, as the final ordaining figure, necessarily closes a series of which it is properly the end, and opens another one. This passage from one series to another effects a metaphorical glide rather than a qualitative leap or a valorization: one does not go from a lesser pleasure to a higher one.

For indeed, between the different moments that the analysis has isolated, there is in circulation but a single central metaphor (the harem) that is filled to saturation levels by a succession of themes.

Each of the series is a different actualization of this metaphor, but, in every instance, it is its expressed totality. Viewed separately, each series exhausts (saturates) the metaphor. The contiguity of the diverse series, for its part, proceeds from an external necessity: that of the reconstructed phantasmic script.

This tireless renewal in a varying register indicates first that the phantasm always exceeds the sum of its actualizations: it is never a completed suite. Second, it indicates that *expenditure* is the nature of the phantasm.[25]

And so the series "almehs and bayaderes" follows the "rituals of the harem," but it does not flow from it, in the strict sense of the term. One should rather say that it is a reprise of it without any prior attempt at determining losses and gains. It would be more accurate to say that it *displaces* it.

Transient guests of the harem, the almehs and bayaderes animate this locus of enclosure with their songs and dances, bringing much needed distraction to its inhabitants who, for the occasion, shake off their languor and set aside the appointed tasks of their idle existence.

Coming from the outside into the hotbed of sensuality that is the harem, the almehs and bayaderes introduce a dimension of playfulness.

As an exercise of the body, dance gives it a physical outlet. It rouses it from its vegetative torpor to maintain it as a body-for-pleasure. As the expression of wantonness through movement, dance prolongs and perfects the erotic delirium through its rythmic and varied figures and its airy shimmer.

As an exercise of the voice, song animates a hushed world of whispers and sighs. It fills it with sonorous bursts and gives it a supplement of soul necessary to the sustenance of a life that otherwise may have appeared arrested or frozen in death. But there is also a lasciviousness of the voice, all suggestiveness and revealing inflections, underscored or punctuated by the play of instruments.

It is the exultation of a body caught in the net of a generalized sensuality, imposed by the idea of the harem, that is expressed in magnified form through the almehs and the bayaderes.

But song and dance, by the very fact that they propel and animate, that is, exteriorize, have the virtues of a psychodrama played out in a closed environment. They are the equivalent of an imaginary escape from the rigid limits of the confinement, distended as long as the feast lasts.

Doubly determined, the theme of the almehs and the bayaderes links up with the other themes without blending with them. Like them, it defines, without stopping it, the migrating meaning of the phantasm of which it is a construction.

This feast of the body is, first of all, a show for only one individual: the viewer-voyeur, namely the photographer.[26]

The exclusiveness that he arrogates unto himself, and which privatizes the feast, makes the photographer the sole owner of a closed space from which he absconds since he is nothing but gaze. For indeed, how is the voyeur to be defined if not as a gaze without presence or a gaze against a backdrop of absence?

48. - ALGER. - Mauresques, costume d'intérieur - Danse des Almées

Algiers. Moorish women in housedress.
Dance of the almehs.

566 A   Mauresques. — ND Phot.

Moorish women.

This double withdrawal—the *clôture* of the locus and the invisible observation point—defines the nature of the phantasmic locus as one of great rarefaction.

The dancers and musical performers do not appear in front of an audience. Rather, they perform the obligatory figures of a *ritual* whose hieratic nature suggests the idea of a place and a feast outside space and time.

As if to emphasize this aspect, here come dancers with their breasts exposed, emerging from the dreamlike fog that is supposed to be conveyed by the soft focus (pp. 93 and 94), linking, in the same suspended gesture, lasciviousness and abandon of the body.

The odalisque may have been the last figure of the series; these half-naked dancers complete it in turn, giving it a special touch, a process of oneiric elaboration, and join with other figures encountered earlier.

The enumeration of the various types of dance (dance of the veil, bellydancing, etc.), the representation of traditional instruments (derbuka, bendir, etc.), the costumes and the props of dance—all of these are subordinated to the necessity of providing folklore, which the postcard cannot escape. This "realism," painstakingly constructed around a few models mimicking dancers and musicians, is no more able than that in the other series to rise above trivial reductiveness.

120. ALGÉRIE – La Danse du Ventre

Algeria. Belly dancing.

Scenes and types. Young woman.

6035 SCÈNES ET TYPES. — Jeune Femme. — LL.

L. Relin. — Alger

323 *Intérieur mauresque · La danse*

J. Geiser, Alger

Moorish interior. The dance.

130 ALGERIE — Danse du Mouchoir

Algeria. Dance of the veil.

Incapable of representing the real feast, the postcard, once again, will be content to evoke it by means of the impoverished signs that constitute its "aesthetics" and its justification. The dancers that it *pins* are akin to the butterflies and insects that museums of natural history and taxidermists exhibit in their glass display cases.

Beyond the ethnographic alibi (folklore), we have a *vivisector's gaze* training itself upon Algerian society. It is the very gaze of colonization that defines, through the exclusion of the other (the colonized), a *naturalness* (the native) that is first circumscribed by the gaze.[27]

It is this same gaze that animates the photographer, that filters through the lens to catch in its aperture a reality that he has already begun to decompose. Photography is a stealer of souls; the "savages" knew this intuitively; and they were yet to suffer a more ferocious and less symbolic spoliation.

The exotic postcard, beyond the folklore it pictures, includes—and that is where the phantasm inhabits it—another component of the colonial gaze, less admissible because more unconscious.

All of this bogus exoticism, this well-tooled suberoticism, would be in vain if it did not unveil what colonization cannot name, even if this unnamed seems to be satisfied with the extreme deformation that the postcard offers it.

The almehs and bayaderes, captured in ridiculous poses without move-

ment—shutter speeds were slow then—
evoke only the dead figures of a ballet
equally forlorn. They do not even have
the grace of faded things. They spin
around, puppets of a tedious and repetitious imagination that is blocked in the
dismal reiteration of its obsessive leit-
motif.

In so doing they reveal the fragments of a truth that, for the time being,
attaches itself to their opulent and impu-
dent bosoms, depicted in a manner calculated to delight a bad taste that is as
brutal as it is pedestrian.

445 SUD-ALGÉRIEN. — La danse

J. Geiser, phot.-Alger.

Southern Algeria. Dance.

271   *Mauresque danseuse*

J. Geiser, Alger

Moorish dancer.

Chapter 9

Oriental Sapphism

This great idleness causes the women to be depraved, and they apply all of their mind to the search for means of distraction.

Jean Thévenot, *Voyage du Levant* (1665)

This rigorous discipline, which turns the harem into a prison, is justified by the passionate disposition of these women, which may impel them to who knows what aberrations.

Alain Grosrichard, *Structure du Sérail*

The favorite theme of a certain French literature, the harem is an ancient obsession the origin of which goes back to the first accounts of travel to the Levant, to the empires of the Great Turk and the Great Moghul. The sixteenth and eighteenth centuries were inexhaustible on the subject of Turkish and Persian mores when it came to the world of the seraglio. More than a simple "scientific" interest was at stake here, as the rich posterity of the theme and its longevity make abundantly clear.

In its association of a political notion (despotism) with a sensual vision (the possession of women), the harem sums up the essence of a certain Levant.

What is remembered about the harem, however, are the sexual excesses to which it gives rise and which it promotes. A universe of *generalized perversion* and of the *absolute limitlessness of pleasure*, the seraglio does appear as the ideal locus of the phantasm in all its contagious splendor.

In the typology of vices and sexual perversions, sapphism is a variant well exploited by under-the-counter literature. But its stake is quite different when it becomes the object of the sexual imaginary. It has the peculiar ability of fulfilling the scopic instinct (voyeurism) without neutralizing or canceling the sexual instinct in the process. It can even stimulate the latter.

Sapphism would thus contribute to further eroticize the idea of the harem, at least as it is constituted in Western belief. It underscores its polysexuality: to male homosexuality, to zoophilia and other vices, one can now add female homosexuality.

But the harem is not merely that. Its extension into the Western imaginary brings other elements into play. It is an erotic universe in which there are no men. This lack of the phallus is eloquently symbolized by the two figures of the High Lord, who can neither enjoy all the women in his seraglio nor satisfy them, and of the eunuchs, who are the absolute negation of the male principle.

Ordered around the absence of the phallus, which it proclaims in its own way, the harem adds another feature to the phantasm: frustration. A locus of no admittance, of taboo (even the gaze is not allowed), it is the perfect emblematic figure. It brings forth and illustrates in exemplary fashion the interplay of pleasure and frustration: their dialectical play dramatized by the fear of castration. The harem is also the locus of the forbidden without appeal: any transgression is paid with loss of life after subjection to the worst torments, applied with cruel refinement.

Bound up with this complex phantasm of the harem, the theme of sapphism could not be avoided by the postcard photographer. His treatment of it is something else altogether.

This series, more so than the preceding ones, has in its favor the advantages of strong erotic connotations. It could become, ultimately, a signified without any signifier. But it cannot do without representation and that leads to its perdition, or rather, to the revelation of what is implicit in it, its repressed.

It is enough for the photographer—in his impatience with the subtlety of nuances—to place side by side two partially naked women, thinking that immediately the idea of sexual perversion will arise and that the lower depths of the libido will be stirred.

The fluster that the photographer wishes to communicate is never in the representation but in its margins. The meaning lies beyond the image, and its elucidation is left entirely to the armchair traveler who fancies this type of card.

The postcard is constantly laying bets on the imaginary of its users. At the same time, it assumes that this imaginary is quite coarse and rudimentary, since it does not attempt to put it to work. The postcard seeks to anticipate the desire of its user and fastens itself to this desire. It never transcends it; it lives in, and from, an osmosis that is its defining characteristic. It knows its clientele only too well; it knows what to give it and especially in

245. — Danseuses des " Ouled Naïl "

'Uled-Nayl dancers.

what form. For a sapphism reduced to its signs, it proposes an unclad proximity and a mutual touching of the flesh.

In doing so, it imposes its own reading standards, but they are quite rudimentary. Since it is addressed to illiterates, as the spelling and the clumsy, repetitious allusions of the senders make clear, the postcard proposes a remedial course in elementary eroticism spiced with a liberal pinch of narcissism. It does not merely propose this course; it cannot get out of it or beyond it. It constitutes all of its riches, and it is summed up in it.

Whether they are standing and clasping each other (p. 97), or reclining against each other (pp. 99 and 100), or arranged in such a way that their breasts eye each other (p. 102), the young women who pose as lesbians have quickly exhausted the imagination of the photographer and the meager resources of the studio.

All the "erotic" repertory of these postcards can be summed up as follows: a hasty pose, embellished with breasts that are raised by uplifted arms.

Meaning stops dead in its tracks, mired on the surface. Commentary stumbles against the shabbiness of such infra-pornography. And yet, at the very time that the postcard photographer was operating, eroticism had found an adequate and far from complacent adjunct in photography.

The colonial postcard is, by its very nature, unsuitable for elevation to such a "high" position: it has too much contempt for its exotic subject to give it anything but a distorting mirror in which it forces it to look at itself.

When a model smiles in these cards, one is not sure whether it is on command, as on p. 97, or at the riduculous salacity of the shot in which she is posing (p. 103). Most often, the facial expression is vague, distant, absent, or vacuous, not even dreamy (p. 100). As if the models themselves had no illusion about the effect they would produce. Or as if they understood that only their breasts could find favor with the photographer and his clients. Reduced to what is enticing about them, these young women can only efface themselves behind their own breasts, which they push forward to earn better payment. Preoccupied with setting up his shot behind the black veil of his camera, the photographer has failed to notice this withdrawal which his plate has captured and preserved. In any case, he does not want to see it. He cannot see it if he is to continue.

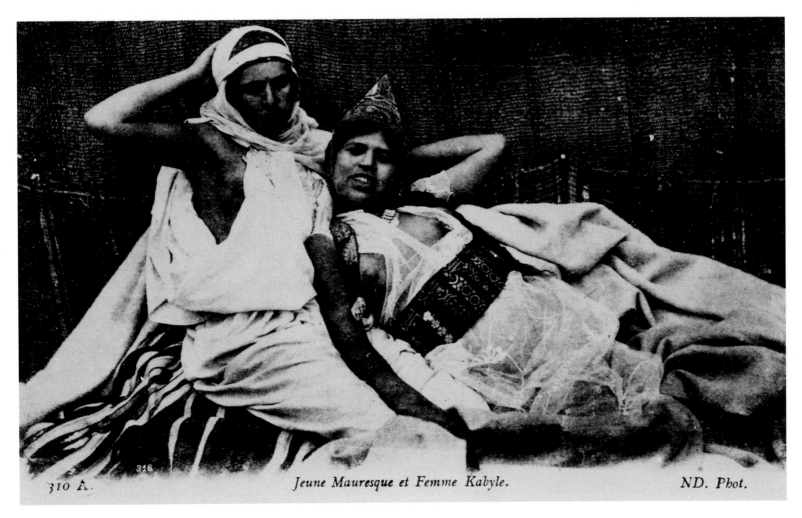

Jeune Mauresque et Femme Kabyle. ND. Phot.

Young Moorish woman with Kabyl woman.

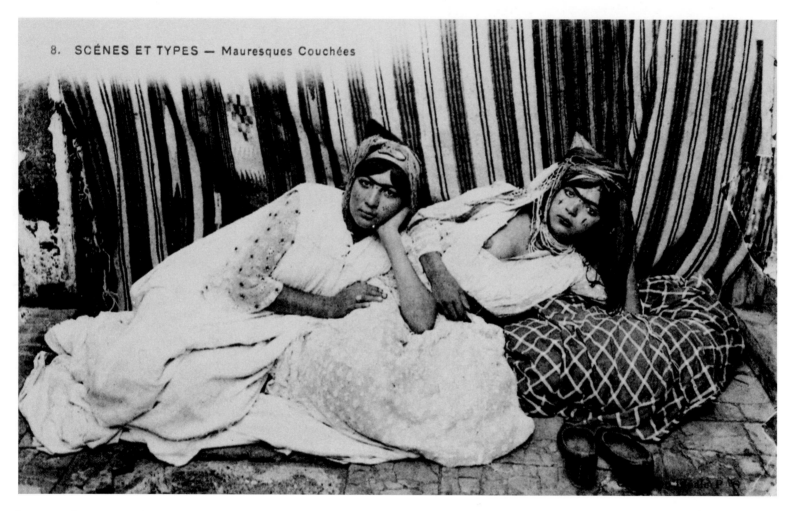

8. SCÉNES ET TYPES — Mauresques Couchées

Scenes and types. Reclining Moorish women.

Collection Idéale P. S.

91. SCÈNES ET TYPES — Jeunes Mauresques

Scenes and types. Young Moorish women.

101

Algeria. Moorish women.

Of all these images, the only one that perhaps stands out, represents two *filles*, one of them lighting her cigarette from the other's lips. At a distance, capturing all that is perturbing in this kiss exchanged by the two women, the photographer, for once, holds back and does not have recourse to his pornographic devices: the breasts remain covered (p. 104).

But this sapphism, whose pseudo-Oriental origin is proclaimed through the mediation of postcards, has another meaning that the photographer links much more explicitly to Algerian society.

These women, posing as lesbians, are pushed toward a generality that is enhanced by their anonymity. These models, without individual identity, become exemplifications of their place. What they proclaim quite unwittingly, since they never master the meaning that the photographer extracts—hence the violence—is that all Algerian women are like this image: lascivious and dedicated to the joys of sapphism and exhibitionism.

It is this effect of contamination that gives the colonial postcard its pernicious noxiousness.

It remains for us to determine the reasons that command this generalization and to ensure that the phantasm of the harem is only a transparent and convenient mask behind which is hidden an even more sordid meaning, the key to which is colonization.

Scenes and types. Young Moorish women.

Moorish women of Algiers.

Chapter 10

The Colonial Harem: Images of a Suberoticism

(Photography) leads me to distinguish the "heavy" desire of pornography from the "light" (good) desire of eroticism.

Roland Barthes, *Camera Lucida*

The figures of the harem are not infinite, whereas the quest for the harem is: it belongs to obsession.

Never has this feature, the obsessive in and of the postcard, been expressed as vehemently and as abundantly —bared so to speak—as in the present series, dedicated to the exhibition of breasts.

We have here the equivalent of an anthology of breasts. And an anthology aims at exhaustive coverage, so the viewer gets to know a large variety of bosoms: first the Beduin, then the Kabyl, then the 'Uled-Nayl, and so on. There emerges from this anthology a sort of half-aesthetic concept: the Moorish bosom, the exclusive property of the exotic postcard, which sets down its canon.

Generally topped off with a smiling or dreamy face, this Moorish bosom, which expresses an obvious invitation, will travel from hand to hand to reach its destination. All along the trajectory, from sender to addressee, it will be offered to view, without any envelope to ensure the intimacy of a private correspondance.[28] Even after its arrival, it will be solicited whenever the *colony and its indiscreet charms* are evoked.

The use of this type of postcard cannot be entirely foreseen: it goes from jocular smuttiness between correspondants ("The lucky bastard! He sure doesn't get bored over there!") to lover's stratagem (the soldier who wants his girlfriend to believe that temptations are numerous) and includes the constitution of comparative "knowledge" (the Moorish bosom compared with the Asian). To these various uses, one must add the periodic report on one's physical and mental health sent

105

to sundry relatives: "I send you these few lines in order to bring you up on what has been happening to me."

Given the range of possible uses, and to satisfy somewhat all the tastes of his faithful and extensive clientele, the photographer will operate in all registers: the exhibition of breasts will be carefully considered.

Three variants order this ensemble. First, the "artistic" variant: it requires that between the breasts and the eyes there be interposed some gossamer fabric that leaves visible the curves of the bosom. Here the photo maintains an ambiguity between modest reserve and whispered beckoning. Flimsily covered by gauze or tulle, and posing in backlight (to ensure the graphism of her form), the model will be shown wearing her jewels to better suggest intimacy, the very intimacy in which the entire "scene" is bathed and to which the viewer is invited.

The second variant could be characterized as that of *roguish distraction*. Troublesome and shameless, one of the breasts, sometimes both for good measure, takes advantage of an opening in the clothing to peek out and parade its nipple under the nose of the spectator. Still in this variant, it may happen that the weight of the breasts is sufficient to open the bodice and thus to permit a view from above upon a well-endowed bosom. What was only half-suggested in the first variant becomes half-explicit here. The garments and the jewels are still present but only as accessories to the operation of showing off: they are the setting in which the breast is displayed. Incidentally, this variant insists on the *practical* side of the clothing of these ladies. Pieces of cloth held with clasps, bolero jackets unencumbered by buttons, transparent and low-cut bodices—these are the elements of an attire of *permissiveness*, which avoids the brassiere, the high-necked blouse, and other constraining trifles. This suggestive and unstable looseness of appearance becomes a component of pornography, but it matters little to the photographer.

The third variant could be familiarly called that of the *display*. The bust, at last freed from the garments designed only to be removed, offers itself either with arrogance or with submissive humility. Accessories are reduced to the absolute minimum: sometimes a few jewels hang from the neck to the breasts. Most often, the breasts are the only ornament of the model. This variant does have the merit of putting an end to any "artistic" reverie on the part of the spectator: the evidence speaks for itself. It also brings commentary to a halt.

Collection Idéale P. S.
89. SCÈNES ET TYPES — Jeune Mauresque

Scenes and types. Young Moorish woman.

97. Scènes et Types — Mauresque

Collection Idéale P. S.

Scenes and types. Moorish woman.

108

135 T   *Bédouine*

                                    ND Phot   Beduin woman.

250 Femme de l'Extrême-Sud Oranais

J. Geiser, phot., Alger.

Woman from the Far South of the Oran District.

Some features are nonetheless shared by all three variants. To begin with, they are all captioned as if they are innocent family portraits. The word *bust*, so often reiterated, is itself connoted to such an extent by its pictorial referent that it ceases to be, through a sort of prophylaxis, the synonym of *bosom* or of *breasts*. The photographer operates in the vast category of the "nude," no longer the preserve only of painters and sculptors. From the technical point of view, all the photographs are taken in medium shot. There is only one full-length portrait (p. 109); this exception confirms the rule that the focus be set on the breasts and nowhere else.

Three captions deserve comment by the heavy and licentious complicity they establish, which duplicates soliciting by an invitation of the kind: "Want to party, honey?" The first of these captions (p. 114) is "Contemplating." The card represents a young woman contemplating her breasts as if to orient the viewer's gaze toward what she herself already admires in an almost amorous fashion.[29]

Moorish woman from Constantine.

Algiers. Moorish woman in housedress.

658 Mauresque d'Alger, costume d'intérieur

J. Geiser. phot.-Alger.

451 Mauresque d'Alger

Algiers. Moorish woman.

Contemplating.   105   En contemplation

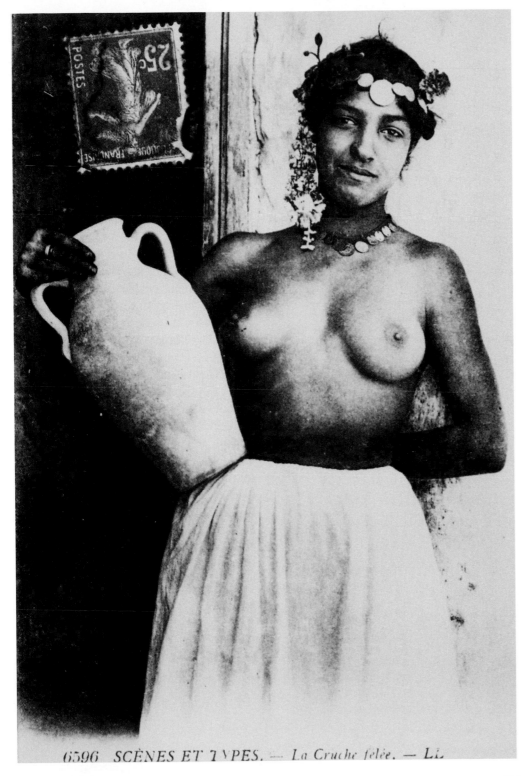

6596 SCÈNES ET TYPES. — La Cruche fêlée. — LL

Scenes and types. The Cracked Jug.

115

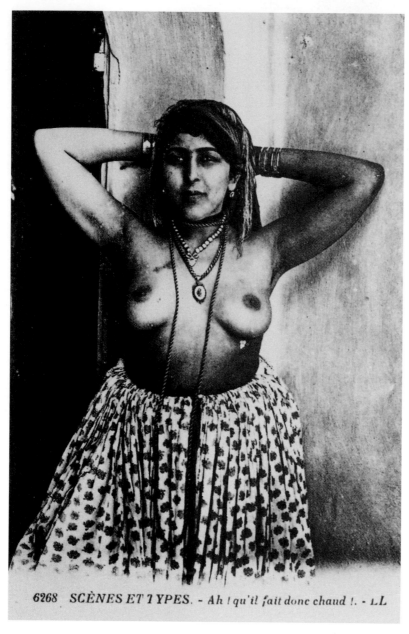

6268 SCÈNES ET TYPES. - Ah ! qu'il fait donc chaud !. - LL

Scenes and types. Oh! Is it ever hot!

The second caption reads: "The Cracked Jug" (p. 115). The model does hold a jug balanced on her right hand, but the jug is quite undamaged! The pictorial reminiscence meant to be recalled by the card is a wink of collusion for barracks denizens.

As for the third card, which represents a woman, somewhat more mature than the others, her hands clasped behind her head in a gesture designed to uplift her breasts, it is captioned with the same disarming humor: "Oh! Is it ever hot!" (p. 116).

This series, whose aims and concerns are so obvious, uses particularly attractive models. The great beauty of some of them could lead one to feelings of nostalgia accompanied by a posthumous tribute to the art of the photographer. In fact, such an "aestheticizing" temptation has not failed to give rise, here and there, to some such undertakings, attempting to capitalize on a few very rare exceptions. The extraordinary portrait on p. 121 or the fantastic surrealism of the postcard on p. 126 might be the figures of such a temptation if we could but forget their end.

6522 SCÈNES ET TYPES. — Ouled-Naïl. — LL.

Scenes and types. 'Uled-Nayl.

6389 SCÈNES ET TYPES. — *Mauresque*. — LL.

Scenes and types. Moorish woman.

It is on "accomplishments" of this sort that a lucrative business of speculative card collecting has been built and continues to thrive. It is also by means of this type of "accomplishment" that the occultation of meaning is effected, the meaning of the postcard that is of interest to us here.

Summarily, and in its customarily brutal idiom, the colonial postcard says this: these women, who were reputedly invisible or hidden, and, until now, beyond sight, are henceforth public; for a few pennies, and at any time, their intimacy can be broken into and violated. They have nothing to hide anymore, and what they show of their anatomy—"eroticized" by the "art" of the photographer—is offered in direct invitation. *They offer their body to view as a body-to-be-possessed*, to be assailed with the "heavy desire" characteristic of pornography.

It is not enough for the colonial postcard to be the rowdy form of this soliciting in public places; it must also be the deceitful expression of symbolic dispossession. The model, in selling the image of her body (dispossession through remuneration), sells at the same time, by virtue of her exemplariness, the image of the body of Algerian women as a whole (extended dispossession).

5576 SCÈNES ET TYPES. — Jeune Femme du Sud Algérien.

LL

Scenes and types. Young woman from the
Algerian South.

119

But the postcard is also one of the illustrated forms of colonialist discourse, its chatty and self-satisfied imagery. In and of itself, it does not speak (it is a photograph of unrelieved flatness, completely summed up by, and in, its surface): *it is spoken*. Its meaning resides elsewhere; it comes from outside itself. It preexists the postcard, but the card gives it a form (the elementary image) that extends it. What it says in its idiom (that of the icon) has already been said by other means, much more brutal and more concrete: the means of operative colonialism.

A ventriloquial art, the postcard, even—and especially—when it pretends to mirror the exotic, is nothing but one of the forms of the aesthetic justification of colonial violence. Such a status of infeudation is constitutive of the postcard.

A form of degraded art, since it is never present in what it represents and, as a result, is without specific finality, the postcard derives from colonial discourse its only, rather shabby, justification. Its constitutive illegitimacy turns it into a hollow and malleable form filled with a discourse that it proceeds to amplify by disseminating it widely but in front of which it effaces itself. Hence its duplicity.

Another version of this duplicity, the discourse that underlies it and forms its armature, is presented as a fragmented discourse through the partial and isolated illustrations that it provides of it. It scrambles its meaning through repetitions and reiterations; it misleads attempts at deciphering it through aesthetic "accomplishments." But though it be an atomized rerun of this discourse, it is, in each instance, its total and accomplished expression, its ever renewed reiteration.

When, as here, it exhibits the body of the *algérienne* laid bare, the postcard obeys another injunction of the same colonial discourse: the injunction of the repressed. The postcard authorizes and ensures *the return of this repressed*; it is its ideal mediation since it does not surround it with any clandestinity; on the contrary, it displays it everywhere and draws all eyes to it.

Scenes and types. Moorish woman.

The postcard is an immense *compensatory undertaking*, an imaginary revenge upon what had been inaccessible until then: the world of Algerian women. Imprinted on the cards, they are the figures of a Parousia: they are reborn, but this time they are available and consenting, welcoming and exciting, submissive and possessed. The postcard can represent them in this way, runs the rationalization, because that which established and maintained the prohibition around them, namely male society, no longer exists. The imaginary abolition of prohibition is only the expression of the absence of this male society, that is, the expression of its defeat, its irremediable rout.

Offered up, body and soul, these *algériennes* are the metaphorical equivalent of trophies, of war booty. *The raiding of women has always been the dream and the obsession of the total victor. These raided bodies are the spoils of victory, the warrior's reward. In this case, the postcard is an enterprise in seduction directed to the troops, the leering wink in the encampments.*

Better yet, displaying, as it does, the traces of this imaginary achievement in the very midst of the society it is "photographing" (the vanquished society), the postcard is the blustering proclamation of the victory bulletin, the final trumpet flourish.

Raided, possessed but always offered with the bonus of a smile and elegance, these women are phantasmically freed by the postcard from their prison, the harem.[30] The postcard lifts the veil from them and grants them a space (that of the postcard) in which they can romp and frolic to their hearts' desire.

But this space, transparent now, where bodies are taken without any possibility of refusal, where they abandon themselves even more if that is possible, is the *very space of orgy*: the one that the soldier and the colonizer obsessively dream of establishing on the territory of the colony, transformed for the occasion into a bordello where the hetaeras are the women of the conquered, these *algériennes* whom the postcard in its guise as a good and wise madam offers for *selection*.

The harem has become a brothel: it is the last avatar but also the *historical truth* of an Orientalism the presuppositions of which are no longer masked by the postcard. Moreover, it displays them and sends them touring. It underscores their meretricious tendencies. Colonialism is indeed the final morality of Orientalism and exoticism. But it is the morality of a procurer and a bawd.

Voyeurism turns into an obsessive neurosis. The great erotic dream, ebbing from the sad faces of the wage earners in the poses, lets appear, in the flotsam perpetuated by the postcard, another figure: that of *impotence*.

Scenes and types. Moorish bust.

123

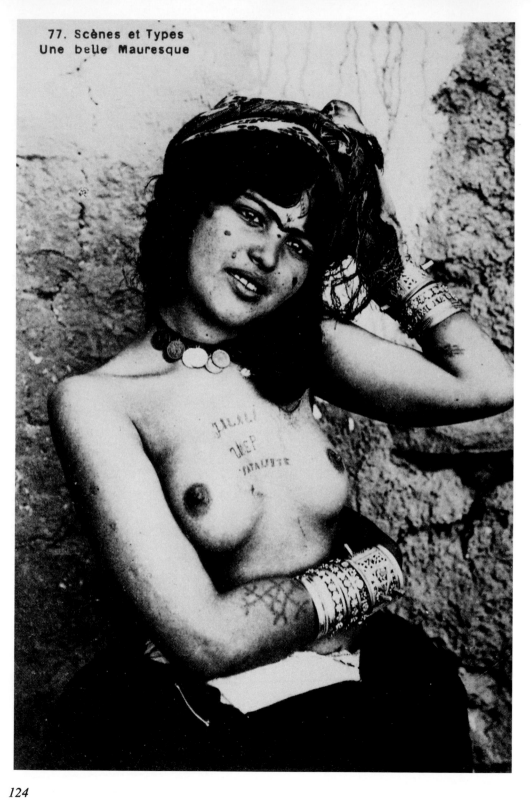

Scenes and types. A beautiful Moorish
woman.

Notes

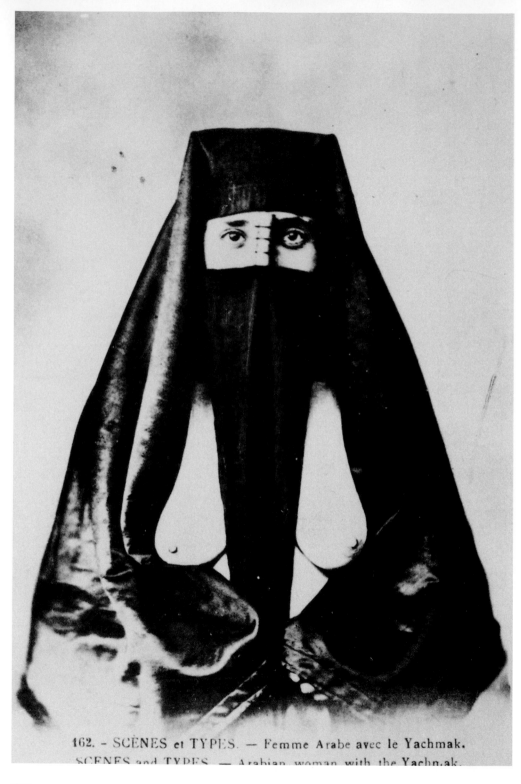

162. - SCÈNES et TYPES. — Femme Arabe avec le Yachmak.
SCÈNES and TYPES. — Arabian woman with the Yachmak.

Scenes and types. Arabian woman with
the Yachmak.

126

Notes

Introduction

1. PierNico Solinas, ed., *Gillo Pontecorvo's The Battle of Algiers* (New York: Scribner and Sons, 1973), pp. 71–72.

2. Frantz Fanon, *A Dying Colonialism*, trans. Haakon Chevalier (New York: Grove Press, 1967), p. 63.

3. See Pierre Bourdieu, *Outline of a Theory of Practice*, trans. Richard Nice (Cambridge: Cambridge University Press, 1977), p. 12.

4. See Edward Said, *Orientalism* (New York: Pantheon, 1979); Norman Daniel, *Islam and the West: The Making of an Image* (Edinburgh: Edinburgh University Press, 1966), and *Islam, Europe and Empire* (Edinburgh: Edinburgh University Press, 1967).

5. Not only do accounts of early Arab travelers from the eleventh century onward, including those by Ibn Khaldun, Ibn Jubayr, and Ibn Battuta, provide a provocative view of the West, but they also comment on the politics and mores of the Western world, particularly since the nineteenth century when cultural and educational exchanges between Europe and the Arab world became common. For surveys of this material, see Ibrahim Abu-Lughod, *The Arab Rediscovery of Europe* (Princeton: Princeton University Press, 1963), and Albert Hourani, *Arabic Thought in the Liberal Age* (London: Oxford, 1970). Modern Arabic literature also reflects strongly the influence of Europe and the West, and novels such as Tayeb Salih's *Season of Migration to the North* (London: Heinemann, 1968) draw on this exchange for their topos and intrigue.

6. Albert Camus, *Actuelles III* (Paris: Gallimard, 1958), p. 63. My translation.

7. Ibid., p. 28.

8. Simone de Beauvoir and Gisèle Halimi, *Djamila Boupacha: The Story of the Torture of a Young Algerian Girl Which Shocked Liberal French Opinion*, trans. Peter Green (London: Andre Deutsch and Weidenfeld & Nicholson, 1962), p. 9.

9. Ibid.

10. Ahmed Taleb, "Lettre ouverte à Albert Camus," *Lettres de Prison, 1957*–1961 (Algiers: SNED, 1966), pp. 76–77. My translation.

11. Roland Barthes, *Camera Lucida*, trans. Richard Howard (New York: Farrar, Strauss and Giroux, 1981), p. 21.

12. Ibid., p. 74.

13. Bourdieu, *Theory of Practice*, p. 14.

14. Jacques Berque, "Polygones étoilés," in *De l'Euphrate à l'Atlas*, vol. 2 (Paris: Sindbad, 1978).

15. The current competition for archival and photographic material on the history of Palestine is an important example of such interest.

16. Herodotus, *The Persian Wars*, trans. George Rawlinson (New York: Random House, 1942), p. 3.

17. *The Koran Interpreted*, trans. A. J. Arberry (New York: Macmillan, 1979), p. 100.

18. See N. Coulson and D. Hinchcliffe, "Women and Law Reform in Contemporary Islam," and Elizabeth H. White, "Legal Reform as an Indicator of Women's Status in Muslim Nations," in *Women in the Muslim World*, ed. Lois Beck and Nikki Keddie (Cambridge, Mass.: Harvard University Press, 1978).

19. Gérard de Nerval, "Voyage en Orient," in *Oeuvres complètes* (Paris: Gallimard, 1978).

20. Albert Camus, *L'Étranger* (Paris: Gallimard, 1942). The novel was written in 1939 in Algeria but was not published until after Camus's arrival in Paris.

21. See Sir Richard Burton, *Personal Narrative of a Pilgrimage to al-Meccah and al-Medinah* (New York: Dover, 1964), and A. W. Kinglake, *Eothen* (Nebraska: University of Nebraska Press, 1970).

22. For general but informed histories of the Maghrib, see Abdallah Laroui, *The History of the Maghrib: An Interpretive Essay*, trans. Ralph Mannheim (Princeton: Princeton University Press, 1977), and Jamil M. Abu-Nasr, *A History of the Maghrib* (Cambridge: Cambridge University Press, 1975). Jacques Berque, *French North Africa: The Maghrib Between Two World Wars*, trans. Jean Stewart (London: Faber and Faber, 1967) deals with the French period of Maghrib history.

23. Laroui, *History of the Maghrib*, p. 305.

24. Cited in David Gordon, *North Africa's French Legacy, 1954–1962* (Cambridge, Mass.: Harvard Middle East Monograph Series, 1962), p. 36.

25. Abdelkebir Khatibi, *Le Roman Maghrébin* (Rabat: SMER, 1979), p. 70. My translation.

26. Fanon, *A Dying Colonialism*, p. 39.

27. Cited in a forthcoming work on the production of the colonial subject by Gayatri Spivak. I am grateful for the opportunity to have benefited from presentations of this material in seminars at Wesleyan University, Center for the Humanities, in 1983–84.

28. Ngugi wa Thiong'o, *The River Between* (London: Heinemann, 1965).

29. Fanon, *A Dying Colonialism*, pp. 37–38.

30. André Gide, *Amyntas*, trans. David Villiers (London: The Bodley Head, 1958), p. 40.

31. André Gide, *The Immoralist*, trans. Richard Howard (New York: Knopf, 1970), p. 161.

32. Rachid Boudjedra, *La Vie quotidienne en Algérie* (Paris: Hachette, 1971), p. 13.

33. See Pierre Bourdieu, "The Kabyle House or the World Reversed," in *Algeria, 1960*, trans. Richard Nice (Cambridge: Cambridge University Press, 1979).

34. Cited in Gordon, *North Africa's French Legacy*, p. 32.

35. Abdelkebir Khatibi, *Maghreb pluriel* (Paris: Denoel, 1983), p. 47n.

36. Alain Grosrichard, *Structure du sérail* (Paris: Seuil, 1979), p. 156. My translation.

37. Assia Djebar, *Les Femmes d'Alger dans leur appartement* (Paris: Des Femmes, 1980), p. 37. See also Fatima Mernissi, *Beyond the Veil* (Cambridge, Mass.: Schenkman, 1975), and Fadela M'rabet, *La Femme algérienne* (Paris: Maspero, 1969).

38. Djebar, *Les Femmes d'Alger*, p. 73.

39. Khatibi, *Maghreb pluriel*, p. 47–48.

The Colonial Harem

1. There is a large literature of unequal value on Orientalism in the broad sense. I refer the reader to a good synthesis by Philippe Jullian, *Les Orientalistes* (Paris: Office du Livre, 1977). The clarity of the presentation is supplemented by a remarkable iconography.

2. In *The Language of Psycho-Analysis*, translated by Donald Micholson-Smith, J. Laplanche and J. B. Pontalis define phantasm as an "imaginary scene in which the subject is a protagonist, representing the fulfilment of a wish (in the last analysis, an unconscious wish) in a manner that is distorted to a greater or lesser extent by defensive processes," p. 314. [From the translators: this definition appears under "phantasy" rather than under "phatasm" in the translation.]

3. On the phantasm of the harem, discussed in the light of psychoanalysis and the history of men-

talities, I refer the reader to the work of Alain Grosrichard, *Structure du sérail* (Paris: Seuil, 1979).

4. As proof of what I am stating: in October 1980, a Parisian weekly, quite expert in the shock of images, if not in shocking images, was quite explicit in stating nostalgic regrets when it compared photos of colonial Hanoi with the Hanoi of today, the Vietnamese Hanoi. One more step (perhaps in the next issue) and the Hanoi of the B52 bombings will be the object of nostalgia. Nostalgia has such inconsequences. (*Paris-Match* no. 1639, 24 October 1980.)

5. The postcards gathered here are dated from the first twenty or twenty-five years of the century. They stop circulating after 1930, that is, once their mission is accomplished. Colonial cinema and tourism will take their place.

The bulk of the postcards is divided into two large categories: "Landscapes and Sites" and "Scenes and Types," head and tails of a complex reality into which the postcard introduces its false and simplificatory order. From this point of view, the postcard takes on the appearance of an "inspection tour" by the owner, a balance sheet of accomplishments, an illustrated journal of the progress of civilization.

6. [From the translators: the author distinguishes typographically between Algerian women in their historical reality and in their representation in the postcard. The first is the *Algérienne*; the second is the *algérienne*. Since this typographical convention cannot be maintained in English, we translate the first as the "Algerian woman" and keep the French term for the second.]

7. During the same period, the "Bretonne" and the "Alsacienne," in traditional garb, are not required to display their bosoms on the postcards that represent them, although they are typifications just as much as the Tlemcen woman or the 'Uled-Nayl woman.

8. A strict academic distinction ought to be made between the colonial postcard and the exotic postcard. I would say that the first is the extension of the second through violence. Colonialism is exoticism *plus* violence. On the colonial postcard,

the barrel of the canon sticks out behind the palm tree.

9. In the countryside, where it is worn little or not at all, the veil does not constitute an obstacle in the sense that is meant here. But the harem, which in its phantasmic form haunts the photographer, can be urban only by the refinements and the luxuries it implies. The countryside is another reservoir of types for the exotic postcard.

10. What the postcard proposes as the truth is but a substitute for *something that does not exist*, at least not photographically. If it establishes its existence in such an arbitrary manner, it is because it has been preceded by another arbitrariness: the colonial one. Abstracting itself from the real, the postcard embarks upon a process at the end of which the native no longer exists as such. He or she disappears. Colonialism is also an *attempt at a general disposal of the native, who will reappear in the guise of the colonized*. This reductive itinerary is visible, or better, readable, in the colonial postcard.

11. The *credibility* of the model—the illusion—is undoubtedly one of the more important factors for the existence of the so-called exotic postcard. After all, it is meant to be sent from the colony to the mother country, that is, to a *public incapable of questioning its truthfulness*. Exoticism is always established by the gaze of the other.

12. The accomplishment of desire, or wish fulfillment, is defined as "a psychological formation in which the wish seems to the imagination to have been realised. The products of the unconscious—dreams, symptoms, and above all phantasms—are all wish fulfilments wherein the wish is to be found expressed in a more or less disguised form." Laplanche and Pontalis, *The Language of Psycho-Analysis*, p. 483 [translation slightly modified].

13. The meaning of *studio* here is a notion of somewhat wider extension than in current usage. It is the use of the model (her physical presence) that constitutes the studio, and it does so even when the photos are shot in a natural decor (exteriors). It vanishes in its own reality, that is, in nature or landscape, to be no more than a connotation or a reference.

14. To say that the postcard is the *degree zero of photography* is to say that, though it is of a piece with photography, the postcard relies only upon the latter's capacity to represent reality, its technology. The postcard is also a perverted photography, an inverted one. It is perverted by its apologetic aims. *Meaning preexists the icon*, the representation. For the postcard, photography exists foremost as something that can be manipulated. The card is an empty photo that comes to be filled with a discourse. It is *photographed discourse*.

15. There is nothing accidental or unexpected about this "failure" of the postcard. The colonial postcard is nothing more than an *innocuous* space in which the sexually repressed characteristic of colonialism can surface or pour itself out at any moment. In no way can the accidental be a mode of functioning of the postcard, since it is entirely based on its mastery by means of models and studios.

16. The postcard photographer may be the first victim—the dupe—of his machination, because he is perhaps but the simple executive agent of a *Photography* elaborated outside his studio and without him. He duplicates only the stereotype; that is his *raison d'être*, his whole métier.

17. The photographic exception (the "success" or "achievement" of photography) is sufficiently rare to deserve mention. In this infinite production of images (an entire industry), the law of numbers occasionally manages to produce a happy coincidence, an unexpected happenstance. But such a happy occurrence only draws attention to the irremediably mediocre character of the bulk of the output.

18. All representation is the expression of a distortion. But the distortion introduced by the colonial postcard achieves a certain degree of absolutism. Even its reality is, at the outset, a pseudoreality. But this distortion raises other, much more complex and more theoretical questions. The reader is referred to the recent work of Michel Thévoz, *L'Académisme et ses fantasmes* (Paris: Editions de Minuit, 1980), for all necessary theoretical clarifications.

19. In the rhetoric of images, or rather, in their rhetorical hierarchization, it appears that the snapshot (that is, the fixation of the fugitive) is the bearer of truth par excellence: *it is life captured at the very moment when it dissolves and escapes*. This snapshot quality—instantaneity—is beyond integration into the postcard because it *generates fuzziness*: the moving shot. The postcard, for its part, works in broad and sharp strokes: *it outlines its subject*. All fuzziness is excluded from it. The only fuzziness it allows itself is that of the *soft focus*: the *metaphorical fog*.

20. The postcard as a catalog is the counterpart to numerous monographs illustrated with engravings of Algerian dress and ornament. It repeats them, copies them, as if this would confer upon it some "scientific" seriousness (ethnography).

21. The *passivity* of the model is her seemingly infinite capacity to mimic the original, whose presence she is supposed to illusively recall. Such a passivity defines the good model as a being without individual will and capable of infinite malleability. The initial violence inflicted by the photographer is borne, in all its consequences, by the model. Her image is never her own. She redoubles it with another image which she imposes over it and which masks her.

22. Painting constantly haunts the postcard photographer. He composes his scenes in the manner of still lifes or of tableaux scenes. By this reference to a pictorial model, the postcard admits that it is an *image beyond itself, that is, without originality*. Other images *dispossess it of itself and pull it toward something that is no longer photography but certainly not the equivalent of painting*.

23. [From the translators: the French word *mouquère* connotes both an Arabic woman and a prostitute.]

24. The word *odalisque*, which begins to appear in French at the beginning of the seventeenth century, comes from the Turkish *odaliq*, meaning chambermaid (from *oda* = chamber). Initially a chambermaid or a slave in the service of the women of the harem, the odalisque was metamorphosed by Orientalist painting (see Jean Auguste Dominique Ingres) into the sublimated image of the one enclosed by the harem. This jewel

of the prohibited space is endowed by the Western imagination with a strong erotic connotation. Gérard de Nerval will draw attention to the semantic error in vain: "*Europe gives an erroneous meaning to the term odalisque.*" There is no way of correcting such libidinal investments.

25. This *expenditure* is characteristic of libidinal investment. It is its corollary in compulsion. It is as if from the infinite multiplication of the means of satisfaction (the image) there ought to be expected *the* satisfaction. Whereas the photographer, from one end to the other of the concatenation of images, meets with nothing but illusion. He never gets out of it.

26. It is as if the postcard photographer had been entrusted with a social mission: *put the collective phantasm into images*. He is the first to benefit from what he accomplishes through this delegation of power. The true voyeurism is that of the colonial society as a whole. The postcard photographer is not important as an individual. *He never goes beyond the stereotype.* He is a wage earner of the phantasm. An obscure and scruffy attendant. And, as such, he disappears in anonymity. Hence, in this essay, the recourse to generality: I always speak of *the* photographer and never of photographer*s*.

27. Colonialism is, among other things, *the perfect expression of the violence of the gaze*, and not only in the metaphorical sense of the term. Colonialism imposes upon the colonized society the everpresence and omnipotence of a gaze to which everything must be transparent. *The exercise of power, especially when the latter is arbitrary, cannot permit the maintenance of shadowy zones; it considers them equivalent to resistance.*

The colonial postcard, for its part, fully partakes in this violence. Moreover, it is its narcissistic expression. *Only the colonizer looks, and looks at himself looking.* The colonized is also symbolically blinded: the colonial order takes away from him or her any *right of (over)sight*, beginning with control over his or her own affairs, which are no longer his or her concerns. *He or she has been fired from this activity so that others may practice it.*

28. "The age of Photography corresponds precisely to the explosion of the private into the public, or rather into the creation of a new social value, which is the publicity of the private: the private is consumed as such, publicly." Raland Barthes, *Camera Lucida*, p. 98. The colonial postcard is the seeing and accomplished form of the "publicity of the private." *Only it forgets that it gained access by breaking and entering and perpetrating violence.* The postcard erases the traces of its crime.

The postcard is also the negation of intimacy. Much could be said here about its exhibitionism as well as about that of its clientele.

Viewed and visible, the postcard is also seeing. Its two faces complete each other. Its reflecting face (recto) and its blind face (verso) are both spaces of saturation: here the chit-chat, there the redundant signs of representation.

No envelope can contain a postcard. Hidden, it immediately ceases to be.

29. This redoubling of the gaze is rather surprising in such a mediocre series. Superimposing upon the same surface the narcissism of the model with the voyeurism of the spectator makes them complementary.

It is strange that in this way an articulation that has nothing obvious about it is apprehended. Such a happenstance of theoretical chance in no way absolves the pornographic aim.

30. A resurgence of this phantasm of liberation occurred on a fine 13 May 1958 when a blunt *généralesse* proposed to Algerian women that they seek their liberation *within* France by dropping the veil. She was, of course, surrounded by troopers. She had forgotten, however, that her veil trick had been understood for over half a century, not an altogether negligible period. But colonialism knows no history.

Selected Bibliography

Selected Bibliography

Alazard, Jean. *L'Orient et la peinture française au XIXème siècle, d'Eugène Delacroix à Auguste Renoir*. Paris: Plon, 1930.

Barthes, Roland. *Camera Lucida*. Translated by Richard Howard. New York: Hill and Wang, 1982. (French original: *La Chambre claire. Note sur la photographie*. Paris: Editions du Seuil, 1980.)

D'Astorg, Bertrand. *Noces orientales. Essai sur quelques formes féminines dans l'imaginaire occidental*. Paris: Editions du Seuil, 1980.

d'Huart, A. and N. Tazi. *Harems*. Paris: Editions du Chêne, 1980.

Gautier, Théophile. *Voyage pittoresque en Algérie* (1845). Geneva: Droz, 1973.

Girardet, Raoul. *Le Temps des colonies*. Paris: Berger-Levrault, 1979.

Grosrichard, Alain. *Structure du sérail. La Fiction du despotisme asiatique dans l'Occident classique*. Paris: Editions du Seuil, 1979.

Jullian, Philippe. *Les Orientalistes*. Paris: L'Office du Livre, 1977.

Laplanche, J. and J. B. Pontalis. *The Language of Psycho-Analysis*. Translated by Donald Micholson-Smith. Norton, 1973. (French original: *Vocabulaire de la psychanalyse*. Paris: Presses Universitaires de France, 1967.)

Lucas, P. and J.-C. Vatin. *L'Algérie des anthropologues*. Paris: Maspéro. 1975.

Maurel, Christian. *L'Exotisme colonial*. Paris: Laffont, 1980.

Metz, Christian. *Le Signifiant imaginaire*. Paris: Bourgois, 1977. *Psychanalyse et cinéma. Communications* 23 (1975).

Said, Edward. *Orientalism*. New York: Pantheon, 1978.

Sibony, Daniel. "L'Image brûle." *Analytiques* 3 (1979):3–7.

Sontag, Susan. *On Photography*. New York: Farrar, Strauss and Giroux, 1977.

Soustiel, J. and Lynne Thornton. *Mahmals et Attichs. Peintres et voyageurs en Turquie, en Egypte et en Afrique du Nord* (Exhibition catalog, 1975).

Thévenot, Jacques. *Voyage du Levant*. Paris: Maspéro, 1980.

Thévoz, Michel. *L'Académisme et ses phantasmes*. Paris: Editions de Minuit, 1980.

Turbet-Delof, Guy. *L'Afrique barbaresque dans la littérature française au XVIème et XVIIème siècles*. Geneva: Droz, 1973.

Verrier, Michelle. *Les Peintres orientalistes*. Paris: Flammarion, 1979.

Malek Alloula, an Algerian writer now living in France, has published several volumes of poetry in French. *Le harem colonial* was first published in France in 1981.

Myrna Godzich is translator of two books forthcoming from Minnesota: Alan Touraine's *Return of the Actor* and Predrag Matvejevitch's *The Poetics of the Event*.

Wlad Godzich teaches comparative literature at the Université de Montréal and at the University of Minnesota, where he is director of the Center for Humanistic Studies, and is co-editor, with Jochen Schulte-Sasse, of the series Theory and History of Literature.

Barbara Harlow is assistant professor of English at the University of Texas at Austin; she is also author of a forthcoming book, *Resistance Literature and Literary Theory* (Methuen, 1986).